R|D|A®

RESOURCE DESCRIPTION & ACCESS

AND

CARTOGRAPHIC
RESOURCES

Y0-CBB-600

ALA Editions purchases fund advocacy, awareness, and accreditation programs for library professionals worldwide.

RDA®

RESOURCE DESCRIPTION & ACCESS

AND

CARTOGRAPHIC RESOURCES

PAIGE G. ANDREW

SUSAN M. MOORE

MARY LYNETTE LARSGAARD

An imprint of the American Library Association
CHICAGO   2015

© 2015 by the American Library Association.

Printed in the United States of America

19 18 17 16 15   5 4 3 2 1

Extensive effort has gone into ensuring the reliability of the information in this book; however, the publisher makes no warranty, express or implied, with respect to the material contained herein.

ISBN: 978-0-8389-1131-0 (paper)

Library of Congress Cataloging-in-Publication Data

Andrew, Paige G.
    RDA and cartographic resources / Paige G. Andrew, Susan M. Moore, Mary Larsgaard.
      pages   cm
      Includes bibliographical references and index.
      ISBN 978-0-8389-1131-0 (alk. paper)
      1. Cataloging of cartographic materials. 2. Resource description & access.
    I. Moore, Susan M., 1960– II. Larsgaard, Mary Lynette, 1946– III. Title.
      Z695.6.A555 2015
      025.3'46—dc23   2014017912

Cover design by Karen Sheets de Gracia. Image © Robert Biedermann /Shutterstock, Inc. Text design by Kimberly Thornton. Composition by Dianne M. Rooney in Minion Pro and Gotham typefaces.

Original illustrations by Barbara Farrell from *Cartographic Materials: A Manual of Interpretation for AACR2* have been redrawn by the publisher for inclusion in *RDA and Cartographic Resources*.

♾ This paper meets the requirements of ANSI/NISO Z39.48-1992 (Permanence of Paper).

CONTENTS

APPENDIXES

FIGURES

CHAPTER 1

THE PAST IS PROLOGUE

BACKGROUND AND INTRODUCTION

RESOURCE DESCRIPTION AND ACCESS (RDA) IS THE LATEST ACCEPTED international standard for cataloging resources in the library profession. It has been through two sets of revisions since it was initially published in 2010 and implemented in 2013. RDA was developed with an eye to bringing library metadata into the wider data universe, and therefore its structure and terminology are a departure from what catalogers are accustomed to under the Anglo-American Cataloguing Rules, Second Edition (AACR2). This new standard will likely continue to evolve based on actual use and subsequent learning outcomes. In fact, the authors needed to update this manuscript after it was first submitted for publication, and they anticipate that some details shared in this book are likely to change as RDA evolves.

The first step in learning something new is to get to know the "lay of the land." When learning to describe—to catalog—cartographic resources using the new standard, it will be necessary to do some things differently, but others will remain the same as in AACR2 or nearly so. Part of this process is to learn and understand a new language, or at least new labels, that identify objects, ideas, and applications. This also means that by instinct catalogers will be comparing RDA instructions with AACR2 rules as they read and use this manual. The authors of this manual are long-time practitioners, and approached learning RDA as it applies to cartographic resources by hanging on to the familiar while investigating the unfamiliar. One overarching piece of advice that the authors can share right up front is this: it's best to learn by doing!

A second step in the learning process is to understand the arrangement of RDA itself. Those who have spent any time cataloging cartographic resources using AACR2 are well aware that its chapter 3 applies to this format. This is the second change between the two standards is revealed. While AACR2 arranges materials by format type, such as monographs, cartographic materials, music, and audio-visual materials, RDA approaches the task by arranging them according to the Functional Requirements for Bibliographic Records (FRBR) and its Group 1 entities: work, expression, manifestation, and item (FRBR 1998; Wikipedia 2013). Note also that another set of FRBR entities is in play within RDA: the Group 2 entities of person, corporate body, and family, or those responsible for the resources being described. Thus, AACR2 rules for description are lumped together at the bibliographic *record* level for formats in Part I, while RDA instructions break out individual elements of description according to where they fit in the FRBR model. In other words, the work we are doing is now at the data *element* level. Because the data elements being described follow from the FRBR Group 1 entities, it is necessary to move to widely different places within RDA to find needed instructions, rather than going to a single location as when using AACR2 rules.

So, what about that new language mentioned previously? The very first instance was just given: AACR2 uses alphanumeric *rules*, whereas RDA uses numeric *instructions*. Why the change in terminology between the two standards? The change is due to the standards themselves: "RDA provides a set of guidelines and instructions on recording data to support resource discovery" (RDA 0.0), while AACR2 provides rules for description and arrangement, or, as stated in rule 0.1, the "rules are designed for use in the construction of catalogues and other lists in general libraries of all sizes." Note also the inherent differences in focus between these two statements. RDA is used for "recording data to support resource discovery," a broad statement of intent and use. In comparison, using AACR2 meant that the goal was to construct catalogs and other lists, a statement with a specific limit of intent. When learning the RDA instructions, this difference will become readily apparent. It will also become clear that when cataloging resources using an evolving RDA, data will live across a variety of information platforms that are no longer focused on and limited to the traditional catalog or finding aid.

What are some of the other new terms a cataloger must learn in order to understand and maneuver within RDA? A non-comprehensive list of terms that might not have exact one-to-one correlations, but in many cases may be understood in that manner, will include:

AACR2	RDA
item	resource
bibliographic record	resource description
cartographic materials	cartographic resources
field and subfield data	element(s)
person, family, or corporate body	entity
[entity characteristics]	attributes
heading	access points
"author"	creator
"added author"	contributor
container	carrier
LC Rule Interpretations (LCRI)	LC-PCC Policy Statements (LC-PCC PS)

Please note again that the terms compared above are not necessarily exact matches because RDA terms tend to be more generalized than AACR2 terms. Practically speaking, however, they are close enough to help catalogers master the words and phrases in this new language that will soon become part of a common RDA cataloging vocabulary.

Another important aspect of this manual has to do with the current cataloging platform most catalogers have been using, the bibliographic utility called OCLC. While RDA itself was built to be platform-independent, the reality is that for now catalogers will continue to use the MARC 21 data content standard and place information in the fields and subfields that make up its structure using OCLC. Forthcoming chapters will describe processes and share examples according to the use of MARC fields and subfields.

The good news is that many things remain the same in practice across these two standards! Such is the case with the two actions that have been performed for decades to craft a bibliographic record: data is either *transcribed* or *supplied,* based on whether or not the needed data is available from the resource in question or from a secondary source. Learning where to find the correct RDA instruction to apply depends on which of these actions is being performed, as well as on the overall arrangement of RDA. So take heart! The basic practical steps remain the same whether crafting a bibliographic record using AACR2 or RDA.

As noted, in AACR2 the rules for describing cartographic items are located primarily in chapter 3. In contrast, RDA is organized so that instructions are spread across parts of five chapters. When using RDA, it is also necessary to consult its introduction for background information and refer to the definitions in a couple of the appendixes. In summary:

AACR2 descriptive rules	=	chapter 3 and primarily appendix B
RDA descriptive instructions	=	chapters 1 through 3, parts of chapters 6 and 7, and appendix B, "Abbreviations and Symbols."

Naturally, in both cases it may be necessary to consult other chapters and appendixes depending on the item or resources being described. When using RDA an instruction may point to other instructions, appendixes, or LC-PCC Policy Statements (LC-PCC PS). Finally, to provide a focus to this manual, the authors assume that the reader:

- has some experience cataloging cartographic resources using AACR2 (although experience is not strictly required)
- is familiar with ISBD punctuation standards
- has used or is familiar with OCLC

In addition, the reader should be familiar with appropriate tools such as *Cartographic Materials: A Manual of Interpretation for AACR2,* Second Edition; OCLC's *Bibliographic Formats and Standards,* and the Library of Congress' *Map Cataloging Manual.* The information and examples in this manual are predicated on full-level descriptive cataloging practice; that is, described at encoding levels I, blank, 1, or L as outlined in either the MARC 21 Format for Bibliographic Data or OCLC's *Bibliographic Formats and Standards.* If catalogers are grounded in these standards and manuals, then they are ready to take those first steps into the world of RDA as it applies to cartographic resources.

OVERVIEW: WHAT TO EXPECT

What are the goals of this manual? First and foremost, this manual is meant to be a "how to" for both experienced catalogers and those who are new or occasional providers of cartographic bibliographic records. It is written, however, at a level that will most benefit those who are only occasionally tasked with providing bibliographic records for cartographic resources or who are brand new to this type of resource. Those catalogers who are well-versed in describing maps and similar resources will also be able to use this manual, though perhaps more selectively. Those who have years of experience cataloging maps, globes, aerial photographs, and the like will use this manual primarily to look up and learn from the RDA instructions when they find themselves in frustrating situations.

In the past several months, the authors have started to learn and apply RDA primarily to cataloging sheet maps, and have concluded that it is not that different from AACR2. To clarify this statement: most certainly, there *are* many differences between the two standards. However, what remains largely the same in crafting a bibliographic description for a cartographic resource is inherent in the nuts-and-bolts process. Scale is determined in the same manner, additional mathematical data is recorded in the same places, the methodology for choosing a primary title when more than one possible title is encountered is the same, and even the practices revolving around sharing correct and accurate measurements for one or more main maps have not changed. Thus, when a cataloger has completed an RDA-based record, it will be apparent that it looks very much like an AACR2-based record, with the exceptions primarily in the details.

Of course there are different practices to be mastered, particularly those that pertain to new MARC 21 fields and subfields for RDA elements. These include the 264, 336, 337, and 338 fields, which will be described in detail later. Another new practice is adding relationship designators to access points to provide information about the relationship or role between the name of the person, corporate body or family, and the resource. These are the *major* changes catalogers will encounter regularly as RDA-based bibliographic records become more common in databases. In particular, the new 33X fields stand out visually.

Of course these are not the only changes. More subtle changes are imposed by this standard primarily to make descriptions more understandable to the users of these records—put another way, to enhance the "readability" of the data—as well as to enhance machine-readability and manipulation of data in general. All are rooted in the principle of user tasks, as set out in the Functional Requirements for Bibliographic Records (FRBR) for bibliographic record data, and Functional Requirements for Authority Data (FRAD) for authority record data. These changes include:

- eliminating most abbreviations, some of which are truly librarian-specific in their makeup and application (e.g., "ms." for manuscript)
- doing away with the arbitrary "rule of three" that was imposed in the era of card catalogs
- changing the use of Latin abbreviated phrases (e.g., "s.n" for "sine nomine") to their spelled-out English or similar translations

In addition, there are similar changes that will be identified throughout this manual.

The authors chose to spend minimal time on the details of FRBR because they felt that by the time this manual was published most readers would be familiar with these models. For those readers who are not, more appropriate resources are available elsewhere. This in no way diminishes the need to learn and understand these two models and the principles they entail, because RDA is based on them. Thus, FRBR and FRAD are key to understanding *why* instructions (formerly called rules) have changed or been added in certain areas, and this is critical to a cataloger's success in learning to apply RDA correctly and fully.

A large portion of the content of this manual is devoted to describing specific RDA instructions and guidelines, and showing how they are applied at the MARC field level. The authors also use illustrations of fields and subfields quite liberally to compare and contrast how a line of information would appear in both the old rules and the new instructions. While this is helpful for understanding specific lines of data, to enhance understanding the appendixes give sample full records to illustrate descriptively the different types of cartographic resources.

Because the purpose of this manual is to provide a concise, pragmatic introduction and overview to using RDA to create bibliographic records for cartographic resources, the authors deal solely with standard cataloging and do not delve into the very important and often complex area of metadata for cartographic resources. The reason for this is that the demand for knowledge about using RDA falls squarely into the midst of cataloging traditional hardcopy cartographic resources, and although the authors will point out instructions pertaining to digital elements, their focus is on assisting where the need is greatest.

Finally, RDA is sometimes silent when it comes to applying instructions in real-world situations due to levels of complexity, or when catalogers lack sufficient data. The standard cannot possibly anticipate every circumstance. Because of this, the reader will find recommendations based on best practices that the authors have applied to cartographic resources over the years. The aim is not to contradict any given instruction or sub-instructions, but to assist the cataloger more fully when the instructions are not sufficiently explicit. Additionally, LC-PCC PSs were established early on to help guide us, although they are aimed at Library of Congress catalogers and members of LC's Program for Cooperative Cataloging (PCC). Even so, there is still room for cataloger's judgment.

This chapter concludes with a brief history of cataloging cartographic resources that lead up to RDA. Chapter 2 introduces the FRBR model as it applies to cartographic resources. These two chapters investigate what remains the same in both RDA and AACR2 applications, and, more importantly, provide a closer inspection of the differences. The heart of this manual, chapter 4, shares RDA field-level details relating to descriptive elements for cartographic resources. The concluding chapter describes relative advantages and disadvantages of the two codes. Finally, the appendixes present a set of documents that can be considered "ready reference" material, including items specific to individual field-level data.

CATALOGING CARTOGRAPHIC RESOURCES: A BRIEF HISTORY

Before examining where we are today, it is necessary to see where we have been. Cataloging of maps in the Western world is thought to have begun at the end of the eighteenth century at the Kurfürstliche Bibliothek (Electoral Library) in Dresden, Germany (Klemp 1982, 22). In the United States, the earliest map catalog was produced at Harvard in 1831; it was arranged by geographic area (Merrett 1976, 3; Drazniowsky 1975, 299). The British Museum's collections, which were first cataloged in 1843 by William Hughes, also used a geographic area arrangement (Merrett 1976, 3). In 1887, Harvard developed a second maps catalog based on subjects. Both Harvard and the British Museum performed recataloging work at the end of the nineteenth century.

In the twentieth century, the Anglo-American cataloging world was distinguished by a succession of codes, beginning in 1908 with the American edition of *Catalog Rules, Author and Title Entries*, compiled by committees of the American Library Association (ALA) and the British Library Association. In this code, the rule is to enter, or "arrange," the description under the cartographer's name if known and otherwise to enter under publisher's name (Hanson 1939, 6–7).

The next code to receive wide use in the United States was *Rules for Descriptive Cataloging in the Library of Congress*, published in 1947. Its section 8 focuses on "Maps, Relief Models, Globes, and Atlases." In 1949, ALA's Division of Cataloging and Classification issued a second edition of Cataloging Rules for Author and Title Entries; section 10A, "Maps and Atlases," begins on page 26. Figure 1.1 shows an example of a bibliographic record created in 1946, before these rules were published. (See Appendix A for a full-map reproduction of a single map sheet from the series cataloged.) Textual sources of information appearing in the margins of the map sheet that are important in the creation of the bibliographic record description for the series are shown in figure 1.2.

In 1967, the first edition of the *Anglo-American Cataloguing Rules* (AACR) was issued, which in its various editions has ruled Anglo-American bibliographic cataloging for many years. Its relatively brief chapter 11, "Maps, Atlases, etc.," had few examples, implied restricted application, and made an attempt to differentiate between works in which a subject aspect dominates and those in which a geographic aspect is primary.

The second edition of the *Anglo-American Cataloguing Rules* (AACR2) was published in 1978, with implementation beginning January 1, 1981. In this interim period, LC's Geography and Map Division began cataloging using what was called "Revised Chapter 6" on April 1, 1978; the rest of LC began using this chapter in September 1974 (Library of Congress 1978, 7). Revised chapter 6 was used because it was

Gt. Brit. War office. General staff. Geographical Section.
   Egypt 1:100,000. [London] : War Office, 1941-
   col. Maps. 44 x 84 1/2 cm. or smaller. (Its [G. S. G. S.] 4085)

Scale 1:100,000.

Set includes various issues of some sheets, some issued by U.S. Army map
   service, some by British Middle East forces (M. D. R. 466) with or without
   series

Designation. Provisional G. S. G. S. 4085.
   "Heights in metres." Vertical interval in contours varies.
   Military grid.

Some sheets with legend and title in English and Arabic.

Shows two classes of railroads, five classes of roads or tracks and five types
   of internal boundaries.

Copied from maps by Survey of Egypt.

Marginal diagrams: [Index to] adjacent sheets ; Markas boundaries.

---

*From a reproduction of Library of Congress card number Map 65-265 in volume 216 of: *The
National Union Catalog, pre-1956 imprints* / American Library Association, Resources and
Technical Services Division. London : Mansell Information Publishing Ltd.; Chicago: American
Library Association, ©1972. Added entries, subject headings, and dashed-on entry for index to
the map series have been excised,

Figure 1.1
**Bibliographic record for the Egypt 1:100,000 map series as created
by the Library of Congress in 1946**

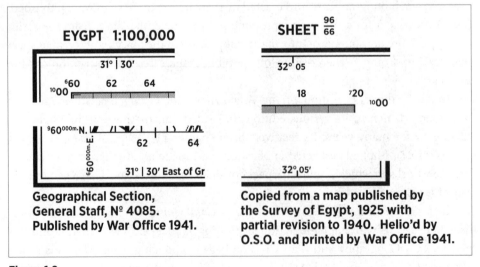

Figure 1.2
"Collar" information from an Egypt 1:100,000 map sheet

based on the International Standard for Bibliographic Description for Monographic Publications (ISBD(M)), which could possibly have contradicted the forthcoming International Standard for Bibliographic Description for Cartographic Materials (ISBD(CM)). Revised chapter 6 incorporated ISBD into the current cataloging practice, a matter primarily of punctuation and in some cases of the order of data. Examples of the latter are:

- inclusion of "author" immediately after title (MARC 245 $c)
- inclusion of publisher immediately after place (MARC 260 $a and $b), even when author and publisher are the same
- inclusion of the numeral "1" prior to the word "map" (when there is only one main map in the entity) to begin the physical description
- the physical description "col." following "map" rather than coming before it

This edition was in many ways a substantial improvement for the map cataloging world, ranging from the new chapter title, "Cartographic Materials," for chapter 3 (a major step forward from chapter 11 in the previous edition), to an expansion of examples and text (Hill 1977), to the chapter itself being enlarged to twenty-seven pages from the original ten. Especially important to map catalogers was the creation of a new field (MARC 255) that gathered scale, projection, and coordinates in one place; under the previous rules, all of these data were given as general notes, with scale receiving a specific MARC field tag of 507 and always appearing as a first note in a list of notes provided. And, after work accomplished by map catalogers, rule 21.1B2 in chapter 21, "Choice of Access Points," which severely limited situations where corporate bodies could be assigned as main entries, was changed by the addition of category "f," which notes that a corporate body given as the main entry is acceptable for cartographic resources. For comparison, an example of the same map series record shown in figure 1.1 is shown using AACR2 rules in figure 1.3.

In response to AACR2, the Anglo-American Cataloguing Committee for Cartographic Materials (AACCCM) was formed in 1979. This international committee included representatives from Australia, Canada, New Zealand, the United Kingdom, and the United States. Their manual, *Cartographic Materials: A Manual of Interpretation for AACR2,* was published by ALA in 1982.

A revised and expanded second edition of AACR2 was issued in 2002, with updates following in 2004 and 2005. The addition of rules covering digital cartographic resources was most important for map catalogers. The new rules for these digital resources were derived from the United States Federal Geographic Data Committee's *Content Standard for Digital Geospatial Metadata* (1998), and dealt with both raster and vector data. Subsequently, a second edition of *Cartographic Materials* was published in 2003 after two decades of work, and was also expanded to cover all forms of cartographic materials.

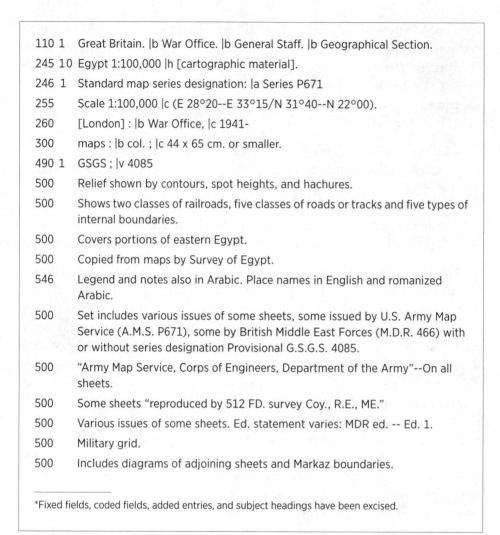

110 1   Great Britain. |b War Office. |b General Staff. |b Geographical Section.

245 10   Egypt 1:100,000 |h [cartographic material].

246 1   Standard map series designation: |a Series P671

255   Scale 1:100,000 |c (E 28°20--E 33°15/N 31°40--N 22°00).

260   [London] : |b War Office, |c 1941-

300   maps : |b col. ; |c 44 x 65 cm. or smaller.

490 1   GSGS ; |v 4085

500   Relief shown by contours, spot heights, and hachures.

500   Shows two classes of railroads, five classes of roads or tracks and five types of internal boundaries.

500   Covers portions of eastern Egypt.

500   Copied from maps by Survey of Egypt.

546   Legend and notes also in Arabic. Place names in English and romanized Arabic.

500   Set includes various issues of some sheets, some issued by U.S. Army Map Service (A.M.S. P671), some by British Middle East Forces (M.D.R. 466) with or without series designation Provisional G.S.G.S. 4085.

500   "Army Map Service, Corps of Engineers, Department of the Army"--On all sheets.

500   Some sheets "reproduced by 512 FD. survey Coy., R.E., ME."

500   Various issues of some sheets. Ed. statement varies: MDR ed. -- Ed. 1.

500   Military grid.

500   Includes diagrams of adjoining sheets and Markaz boundaries.

*Fixed fields, coded fields, added entries, and subject headings have been excised.

Figure 1.3
Bibliographic record for Egypt 1:100,000 map series derived from AACR2

RDA now arrives, and is rolled out to the profession at the 2010 ALA Annual Conference held in Washington, DC. After a year-long test period by catalogers from the Library of Congress, National Library of Agriculture, and National Library of Medicine, along with volunteers from more than twenty other institutions, followed by an evaluation period ending in 2012, RDA was accepted as the next cataloging standard. RDA was implemented in the United States on March 31, 2013. The need for several months of training for LC catalogers accounts for the discrepancy between the formal acceptance and implementation of RDA (Wiggins 2012). Although RDA is a major shift, the ideas behind bibliographic description—creator/author, title, edition, place of issuance, issuing body, date of issuance, and so forth—remain.

As is obvious from the foregoing history of cataloging, our standards have a long history of evolving over time, and RDA is just a next step in a process that itself will probably be followed by new codes. What this history of change means is that records for cartographic and other resources created from several earlier standards will continue to live side-by-side in OCLC and in our local catalogs.

REFERENCES

Anglo-American Cataloging Rules. 1967. Prepared by the American Library Association, the Library of Congress, the Library Association, and the Canadian Library Association. Chicago: American Library Association.

Anglo-American Cataloguing Rules. 1978. Prepared by the American Library Association, the British Library, the Canadian Committee on Cataloguing, the Library Association and the Library of Congress; edited by Michael Gorman and Paul W. Winkler. 2nd ed. Chicago: American Library Association.

Anglo-American Cataloguing Rules. 2nd ed., 1988 revision. Chicago: American Library Association.

Anglo-American Cataloguing Rules, 2nd ed., 2002 revision. Chicago: American Library Association.

Anglo-American Cataloguing Rules, 2nd ed., 2002 revision, 2005 update [loose-leaf volume]. Ottawa: Canadian Library Association; Chicago: American Library Association.

Cartographic Materials: A Manual of Interpretation for AACR2. 1982. Chicago: American Library Association.

Cartographic Materials: A Manual of Interpretation for AACR2, 2002 Revision, Second Edition, 2003. Edited by Elizabeth Mangan. Chicago: American Library Association.

Catalog Rules, Author and Title Entries. 1908. Compiled by committees of the American Library Association and the British Library Association. Chicago: American Library Association.

Drazniowsky, Roman. 1975. *Map Librarianship: Readings by Roman Drazniowsky.* Metuchen, NJ: Scarecrow Press.

Hanson, J. C. M. 1939. *A Comparative Study of Cataloging Rules Based on the Anglo-American Code of 1908: With Comments on the Rules and on the Prospects for a Further Extension of International Agreement and Co-operation.* Chicago: University of Chicago Press.

Hill, J. S. 1977. "Developments in Map Cataloging at the Library of Congress." *Special Libraries* 68 (4):149–54.

IFLA Cataloguing Section and ISBD Review Group. 1974. *International Standard Bibliographic Description for Monographic Publications (ISBD(M)).*

IFLA Cataloguing Section and Section on Geography and Map Libraries. 1987. *International Standard Bibliographic Description for Cartographic Materials (ISBD(CM)).* Revised edition.

London: IFLA Universal Bibliographic Control and International MARC Programme. Also available at www.ifla.org/files/assets/cataloguing/isbd/isbd-cm_1987.pdf.

IFLA Study Group on the Functional Requirements for Bibliographic Records "Functional Requirements for Bibliographic Records, Final Report." 1998. München: K. G. Saur. Available online as an HTML file at http://archive.ifla.org/VII/s13/frbr/frbr_current_toc .htm; available as a PDF file at www.ifla.org/files/assets/cataloguing/frbr/frbr_2008.pdf.

IFLA Working Group on Functional Requirements and Numbering of Authority Records (FRANAR). 2009. *Functional Requirements for Authority Data*. München: K. G. Saur. Also available at www.ifla.org/files/assets/cataloguing/frad/frad_2013.pdf

Klemp, E. 1982. "On the Access to Cartographic Collections in GDR Libraries." *Inspel* 16: 21–30.

Library of Congress. Processing Department. *Cataloging Service Bulletin* 125 (Spring 1978): 7.

Library of Congress. Descriptive Cataloging Division. 1947. *Rules for Descriptive Cataloging in the Library of Congress*. Preliminaryed. Washington, DC: US Government Printing Office.

Library of Congress. Geography and Map Division. 1991. *Map Cataloging Manual*. Washington, DC: Cataloging Distribution Service.

Library of Congress. Network Development and MARC Standards Office. 2013. *MARC 21 Format for Bibliographic Data*. 1999 edition with updates through September 2013. www.loc.gov/marc/bibliographic/ecbdhome.html.

Merrett, Christopher Edmond. 1976. *Map Cataloguing and Classification: A Comparison of Approaches*. Sheffield, UK: University of Sheffield, Postgraduate School of Librarianship and Information Science.

OCLC. 2013. *Bibliographic Formats and Standards*. 4th ed. www.oclc.org/bibformats/en.html.

Resource Description and Access. 2010. Chicago: American Library Association; Ottawa, Ont.: Canadian Library Association; London: Chartered Institute of Library and Information Professionals.

Wiggins, Beacher. 2012. "Library of Congress Announces its Long-Range RDA Training Plan (Updated March 2, 2012): Resource Description and Access at the Library of Congress." http://www.loc.gov/catdir/cpso/news_rda_implementation_date.html.

Wikipedia, s.v. "Functional Requirements for Bibliographic Records." http://en.wikipedia.org/ wiki/Functional_Requirements_for_Bibliographic_Records.

CHAPTER 2

RDA AND FRBR ENTITIES AS APPLIED TO CARTOGRAPHIC RESOURCES

An Overview

WORK-EXPRESSION-MANIFESTATION-ITEM

THE FOCUS OF THIS CHAPTER IS ON THE FRBR GROUP 1 ENTITIES mentioned at the beginning of this book: work, expression, manifestation, and item (referred to as WEMI). This is only an overview; detailed information at the manifestation level for specific elements is provided in chapters 3 and 4.

It is important that catalogers be familiar with using RDA generally; it is also recommended that they read summary works about RDA such as Chris Oliver's *Introducing RDA: A Guide to the Basics*. A useful guide to attributes of the WEMI entities is on page 20 of that text, which notes that attributes of a "work" for a cartographic resource include coordinates, and attributes of an "expression" for a cartographic resource include scale. In addition, as a helpful guide appendix B of this book includes a bibliographic record for a map annotated at the field level that shows which attributes belong to which level of the WEMI model.

Attributes of a manifestation look quite familiar to a cataloger accustomed to using AACR2, because they include publisher/distributor, etc.; date of publication/distribution, etc.; form of carrier; extent of carrier; and more, as do those for an item (e.g., bar code, any marks or inscriptions unique to that item, etc.) because it is highly unlikely that a map cataloger will have the whole print run to catalog. Attributes of work and expression are another matter, because map cataloging under previous codes very seldom used uniform titles, which are analogous to RDA's preferred title for the work and preferred title for the expression, which both appear in MARC field 240.

Most of the cartographic resource titles that catalogers work with have single manifestations, so recording a large number of work or expression attributes when to the best of the cataloger's knowledge there is only one manifestation does not seem to be the best use of a cataloger's time. It is thus not surprising that in US practice at the time this book was written catalogers do not generally make work/expression records. Neither is it the best use of the cataloger's time to hunt extensively for all other manifestations, for example, searching the Internet for a digital version of a paper map being cataloged. Judging from a study of a 2001 instantiation of OCLC's WorldCat database, it may be relatively common for there to be only one manifestation of a work, not only for cartographic resources but for non-cartographic resources as well, with 78 percent of the records in WorldCat having only one manifestation:

> As of December 2001, WorldCat contained 46,767,913 records [rounded to 47 million]. For the purposes of this study and in line with FRBR model definitions, it is assumed that each bibliographic record in WorldCat describes a manifestation. Based on the analysis of the sample, these 47 million manifestations can be traced back to approximately 32 million distinct works in WorldCat. The average work in WorldCat has approximately 1.5 manifestations, indicating that for the most part, works in WorldCat are small, single-manifestation entities. More than 25 million of the 32 million works in WorldCat (78%) consist of a single manifestation. Ninety-nine percent (99%) of all works in WorldCat have seven manifestations or less, and only about 30,000, or 1%, have more than 20 manifestations. (Bennett, Lavoie, and O'Neill 2003, section 4.1 in unpaged online document)

Perhaps the Group 1 entities taken together apply best to literary or fine-art resources; the full model seems not to apply easily or intuitively to all textual resources (e.g., a physics textbook). The last sentence of the FRBR Review Group's "Frequently Asked Questions about FRBR" states: "The whole range of documents from *Hamlet* to self-published holiday recollections represents a continuum from maximal helpfulness of FRBR to no helpfulness at all" (IFLA 2003).

Conversely, cartographic resources are primarily graphic resources that often, but not always, have text on them; for instance, there are remote-sensing images that lack added text. Cataloging graphic resources still has a good deal in common with cataloging textual resources such as author, title, and issuance information; but requires some different approaches in addition to differences in applying instructions.

The primary situations where work/expression is most applicable to cartographic resources are:

- revisions and other editions (including facsimiles); for example, the several revisions of the United States Central Intelligence Agency's (CIA) page-size political map of Africa, as seen in figure 2.1
- the multiple revisions of individual sheets in the United States Geological Survey's 7.5-minute topographic map series at 1:24,000 scale (most notably of urban areas), although the current program, *The National Map*, is aimed at revising all sheets regularly ("U.S. Topo Quadrangles" 2013)

How does the cataloger make clear to users what the various relationships between cartographic resources are? RDA as a whole, and its instructions in detail, emphasize the importance of cataloging in such a way that it is easy and quick for users of an online catalog to view every edition of a given map without confusing it with editions of maps with the same author and title (e.g., all of the CIA maps of Africa).

Translating the RDA instructions into application within the MARC format—which in spite of the work to create a successor seems to be a practice that is likely to be with us for a while—provides some different options. For example, when cataloging a facsimile, the cataloger may use the MARC 534 field to share information about the original; or, if the cataloger were cataloging the original map and knew of one or more facsimiles (as often occurs with well-known pre-1800 maps), the cataloger could use a MARC 533 field to express information about the facsimile. This is especially important because facsimiles in some cases have a title proper that differs from the title proper of the original (i.e., the title within the neat line of the facsimile reproduction), although a title of the facsimile in a margin may be quite different. For example, when published in the United States, facsimiles of maps of the world in a non-English language may have a title proper that is a translation or even just a simplification of the original map's title (e.g., for a map of the world in Latin the translated title might be "map of the world").

One question that quickly comes to mind for an experienced map cataloger who has been using AACR2 is how to deal with cartographic resources that appear in various editions. As noted previously, classic examples include CIA maps of countries, continents, and regions, as well as editions of base-map topographic map series sheets for urban areas. A related question is how to deal with these editions once they have been electronically scanned. In both cases, cartographic content must be a priority. A newer option for a maps cataloger is to use the 775 field for other-edition situations or the 776 field for additional physical format situations. How best to use these two fields for reproductions of resources, including cartographic ones, is still being "tested" by catalogers. For details, see chapter 4; additionally, appendix G shows an example of a record for a facsimile reproduction.

Another query that comes to mind is how to deal with different digital versions of the same hardcopy cartographic resource. The resource can be scanned at different levels of resolution (i.e., 1200 ppi, 600 ppi, etc.), scanned with a scanner (raster form),

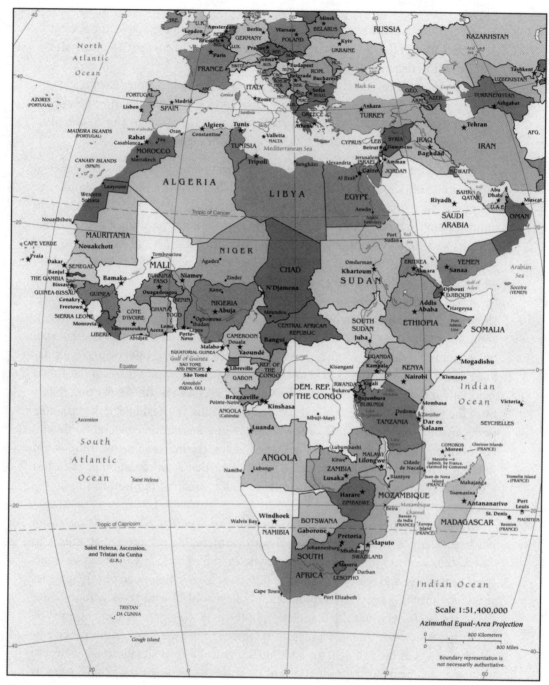

Figure 2.1
Example of a CIA map of Africa

or may have its various layers of information generated in vector form. In addition, the resource may be online, or may be available only on DVD, CD, or a removable hard drive. From an RDA point of view, as long as the content is the same, print and electronic are only different manifestations. This means, ultimately, displaying different but related resources according to a user's request to show all electronic versions of all the editions of a given work, or all the hardcopy versions, using the indexing processes that integrated library systems permit.

ATTRIBUTES OF A WORK AND ATTRIBUTES OF AN EXPRESSION

The attributes of a work that are unique to cartographic resources are:

COORDINATES: degrees, minutes, and seconds of longitude and latitude; for celestial charts, angles of declination and ascension that form the outer boundaries for the area

EQUINOX: for a celestial chart, the year that is the point of reference for the chart (FRBR 2009, 35)

The attributes of an expression that are unique to cartographic resources are:

SCALE: distance as represented on the resource compared to actual distance represented on the ground

PROJECTION: mathematical constructs used to represent a geographic surface that is three-dimensional on a two-dimensional surface

PRESENTATION TECHNIQUE: the "method used to represent geographic or other features in a cartographic image (e.g., anaglyphic, diagrammatic, pictorial, etc.)"

REPRESENTATION OF RELIEF: the "technique used to depict the elevations or the inequalities of a land surface or of the bed of a body of water in a cartographic image (e.g., contours, shading, hachures, spot heights, bathymetric tints, soundings, etc.)"

GEODETIC, GRID, AND VERTICAL MEASUREMENT: the "information on the spheroid used to construct the cartographic image, the grid or referencing systems used in the image, horizontal datum, vertical datum, mathematical data on contour intervals, bathymetric intervals, etc."

RECORDING TECHNIQUE: for a remote-sensing image, the remote-sensing technique used to capture the image (e.g., aerial camera, radar, multispectral scanner, etc.)

SPECIAL CHARACTERISTIC: for a remote-sensing image, such information as altitude of the sensor, position of the platform, name of the satellite, cloud cover, etc. (FRBR 2009, 39)

Note that in the United States, aerial photographs are considered to be remote-sensing images, and in FRBR they are not; additionally, in the United States they are "remote-sensing images," whereas FRBR calls them "remote sensing images."

WEMI IN ACTION: SOME EXAMPLES FROM THE WORLD OF CARTOGRAPHIC RESOURCES

Ptolemy's *Geographia/Geography* fits the WEMI model very well. For an example, we will look at a Library of Congress-created bibliographic record (see figure 2.2); note that except for author and subject headings, the record is in pre-AACR2 form.

LC control no.:	map66000857
Type of material:	Cartographic Material
Personal name:	Ptolemy, active 2nd century.
Uniform title:	Geographia. Latin. 1513
Main title:	Geographia. Strassburg, 1513. With an introd. by R. A. Skelton.
Published/Created:	Amsterdam, Theatrum Orbis Terrarum, 1966.
Description:	xxii, [360] p. illus., maps (part fold., part col.) 46 cm.
Related names:	Skelton, R. A. (Raleigh Ashlin), 1906-1970, ed.
Subjects:	Ptolemy, active 2nd century. Geographia.
	Atlases -- Early works to 1800.
	Early maps -- Facsimiles.
	Geography -- Early works to 1800.
Notes:	Facsim. of the copy in the State University of Utrecht Library.
	Errata slip inserted.
	Bibliography: p. xxii.
Series:	Theatrum orbis terrarum; a series of atlases in facsimile, 2d ser., v. 4

Figure 2.2
Example record for Ptolemy's Geographia derived from a bibliographic record in the Library of Congress' online catalog

This is a facsimile of a specific printing of the work. As we look over the record, it appears that the work embodied in this manifestation is represented by the combination of the authorized access point for the creator ("Personal name"), combined with the preferred title for the work:

> Ptolemy, active 2nd century.
>   Geographia.

Scale, as previously noted, is considered to be an attribute of an expression, rather than of a work, but there is no guarantee that each of the expressions in atlas form would be the same size; for example, an expression and its manifestation(s) that were published in a larger format would have a different scale than would an expression and its manifestation(s) published in a smaller format. An additional reason for not including scale in the work record as an identifying attribute is that maps in *Geographia*, like the maps in many atlases, do not necessarily each have the same scale.

Because there are many expressions of this work, it is useful to identify not only the work, but also the expression. The authorized access point representing the expression is constructed by combining the authorized access point for the work and adding significant attributes that will identify and distinguish the expression:

> Ptolemy, active 2nd century.
>   Geographia. Latin. 1513

In this case, two attributes were added: language of expression (RDA 6.11) and date of expression (RDA 6.10). It is often difficult to identify the date of expression, so the instruction (RDA 6.10.1.1) for this element states: "If no specific date can be identified as the date of expression, treat the date of the earliest manifestation embodying the expression as the date of the expression."

There could conceivably be more than one Latin version of *Geographia* that was published in 1513, which is why *Geographia* expressions are generally referred to in the world of cartography by combining place and date of publication (McEathron 2002, 185). In RDA, this information would be understood to be the other distinguishing characteristic of the expression and date of expression. This would perhaps require a change in expression to something like:

> Ptolemy, active 2nd century.
>   Geographia, Strassburg. Latin. 1513

For a detailed discussion on Ptolemy's *Geographia* as a work, see McEathron (2002).

Turning to a different situation, revisions of sheet maps are another prominent example of works of cartographic resources. There are two major instances of this situation: revisions of single monographic maps and map series. Because map series are by far the more complicated of these two situations, the former, revisions of single monographic maps, will be discussed first.

Revisions of single monographic maps are often refreshingly straightforward in that the only differing bibliographic information from each manifestation may be edition and date of publication; place of publication and/or publisher and other data may be the same or may differ from edition to edition. One example that has already

Figure 2.3
CIA map alphanumeric code

been noted are those maps issued by the United States Central Intelligence Agency. Author, title, scale, place of publication, and publisher remain the same from edition to edition of the same map, although it is rare for the creator and imprint data to appear on the map. Because a title of an individual map often will be generic, for example "Africa," it is essential for some other element to differentiate between the various CIA maps with the title of "Africa." The good news is that these particular various versions of cartographic resources do indeed have a code—in small print and in parentheses, in the lower right- or left-hand corner in the margin—that is unique for each work. Figure 2.3 is an example of one of these codes.

For this resource, the work record would be:

> United States. Central Intelligence Agency.
> Africa : (G00392)

If this unique code did not exist, then the cataloger would be in the interesting situation of attempting to differentiate the different works of "Africa" by another method. The various works are differentiated from each other by their scale, and, in their paper form, dimensions. Because scale is considered to be an attribute of expression and physical size an attribute of manifestation, to create the preferred title for the work at a minimum, scale would be used as part of the work record—keeping in mind that the scale expressed as a representative fraction is not appropriate for any digital versions of the work.

After this, matters get more complicated, primarily because of changes in author, title, or both. A relatively simple version of this situation is given as an example in "Cartographic Materials as Works" (McEathron, 188–89). The maps by Robert G. Bailey on the ecoregions of the United States have changed title over time: "Ecoregions of the United States," 1976; "Ecosystems of the United States," 1978; and then back to "Ecoregions of the United States," 1994/1995. How would a cataloger deal with this title change? According to RDA 6.2.2.4, the preferred title for the work would be

"Ecoregions of the United States." The title "Ecosystems of the United States" may be recorded as a variant title for the work; it also remains the title of the manifestation that was published in 1978. Each of these three titles has the same scale (1:7,500,000), so they would qualify as being the same work.

In these situations, where the cataloger has reason to believe that it is indeed the same work, an author (i.e., a different author takes over the map) or title (as in the case of the Bailey maps) may differ, and it becomes tempting not to consider them the same work, while at the same time recognizing that they are related works. Even when later maps—although with differing bibliographic elements—are of the same subject (e.g., topographic maps of an entire state), they may include statements noting derivation from earlier maps that indicate their relationships. For an example of this, see the article by Morse (2012), which provides a thorough discussion of relationships in the world of monographic sheet maps.

Map series have their own special circumstances. Individual sheets in a given map series may be revised, and often more than once. In addition, the way cartography works is that smaller-scale map series are based on the largest-scale map series, which is called the base map. For example, the United States' topographic map series base map is at a scale of 1:24,000; the smaller-scale series—such as the 1:100,000-scale maps—are derived from these large-scale base maps, whether this information is in digital or hardcopy form. For those countries where all scales of the national topographic series have the same title, the nested map series may be considered a work. (This does not generally apply to US national topographic series, where each series has its own title.)

To examine this situation further, consider the relatively simple case of revisions of an individual sheet that has been issued in multiple physical formats, such as a 1:24,000-scale sheet in the US national topographic map series authored and published by the United States Geological Survey (USGS) (see figure 2.4). This example by no means includes all editions and all possible physical formats.

There are some challenges in fitting this into the WEMI model:

1. To make this a unique preferred title of the work, the cataloger has the option of which title to use as title proper, so the MARC 240 could be "7.5-minute series (topographic). $p Goleta, Calif." Or it could be "Goleta, California-Santa Barbara Co." Either of these, in combination with the creator "Geological Survey (U.S.)," would make it a unique preferred title.

2. Moving on to expression records—what about when there is a revision that is available in one or more physical formats? Following the preceding examples, these could be paper, microform, and digital. Because work and expression are about content, and manifestation and item add to that physical format, there would be an expression record for the revision, and then a manifestation record for each of the physical formats.

Geological Survey (U.S.). Goleta quadrangle, California – Santa Barbara Co., 7.5 minute series (topographic).

1950

paper: 3700s VAR .U5 CA 7.5 Goleta Ed.1950

microfilm: 3700s VAR .U5 CA 7.5 Goleta Ed.1950 Film

digital: 3700s_var_u5_ca_75_goleta_ed1950 Available as .jpg ; .tif (29megabytes)

1951

paper:.   3700s VAR .U5 CA 7.5 Goleta Ed.1951

microfilm: 3700s VAR .U5 CA 7.5 Goleta Ed.1951 Film

digital: 3700s_var_u5_ca_75_goleta_ed1951 Available as .jpg ; .tif (29megabytes)

1967

paper: 3700s VAR .U5 CA 7.5 Goleta Ed.1967

microfilm: 3700s VAR .U5 CA 7.5 Goleta Ed.1967 Film

digital: 3700s_var_u5_ca_75_goleta_ed1967 Available as .jpg ; .tif (29megabytes)

1982

paper: 3700s VAR .U5 CA 7.5 Goleta Ed.1982

microfilm: 3700s VAR .U5 CA 7.5 Goleta Ed.1982 Film

digital: 3700s_var_u5_ca_75_goleta_ed1982 Available as .jpg ; .tif (29megabytes)

1976

paper: 3700s VAR .U5 CA 7.5 Goleta Ed.1976

microfilm: 3700s VAR .U5 CA 7.5 Goleta Ed.1976 Film

digital: 3700s_var_u5_ca_75_goleta_ed1976 Available as .jpg ; .tif (29megabytes)

1995

paper: 3700s VAR .U5 CA 7.5 Goleta Ed.1995

microfilm: 3700s VAR .U5 CA 7.5 Goleta Ed.1995 Film

digital: 3700s_var_u5_ca_75_goleta_ed1995 Available as .jpg ; .tif (29megabytes)

Figure 2.4
Examples of various editions of the Goleta, California USGS topographic quadrangle

3. Given that there are more than 57,000 sheets (not editions, just sheets) in this topographic map series (7.5-minute and 15-minute), is it desirable to create up to 57,000 preferred titles for works, one per sheet? Probably not; given that the USGS has moved to revise every sheet in the 7.5-minute series as often as once per year it is not practical unless computers automatically generated work and expressions records for us.

On to the more complicated matter of families of national topographic map series. Our example here is the national topographic map series of Belgium, each series of which has the same title, "Carte topographique de Belgique." Consider such a work record, which covers all scales of the national topographic maps of Belgium as a work. This work would include as expressions all the other maps with smaller scales, even when each has separate subtitles (e.g., "cartographie numérique")—1:20,000, 1:50,000, and so forth (Kalf 2008). Then each of these scales would constitute a different expression.

As can be seen from the foregoing, the application of WEMI to cartographic resources is at this point not an always/never situation. It will take applying the model in many situations to determine guidelines for how it is best used for the purpose of cataloging cartographic resources.

REFERENCES

Bennett, Rick, Brian F. Lavoie, and Edward O'Neill. 2003. "The Concept of a Work in WorldCat: An Application of FRBR/Functional Requirements for Bibliographic Records." *Library Collections, Acquisitions, and Technical Services* 27 (1): 45–59. http://www.oclc.org/content/dam/research/publications/library/2003/lavoie_frbr.pdf.

IFLA Cataloguing Section, FRBR Review Group. October 12, 2009. "Frequently Asked Questions about FRBR." www.ifla.org/VII/s13/wgfrbr/faq.htm.

IFLA Study Group on the Functional Requirements for Bibliographic Records "Functional Requirements for Bibliographic Records, Final Report." 2009. München: K. G. Saur. Available online as an HTML file at http://archive.ifla.org/VII/s13/frbr/frbr_current_toc .htm; available as a PDF file at www.ifla.org/files/assets/cataloguing/frbr/frbr_2008.pdf.

Kalf, Ruth. 2008. "FRBR: An Opportunity for Map Collections and Map Users?" *LIBER Quarterly* 18 (2).

Library of Congress. Online catalog. http://catalog.loc.gov.

McEathron, Scott. 2002. "Cartographic Materials as Works." *Cataloging and Classification Quarterly* 33:181–91.

Morse, Tami. 2012. "Mapping Relationships: Examining Bibliographic Relationships in Sheet Maps from Tillett to RDA." *Cataloging and Classification Quarterly* 50 (4): 225–48.

Oliver, Chris. 2010. *Introducing RDA: A Guide to the Basics.* Chicago: American Library Association.

United States Geological Survey. 2013. "U.S. Topo Quadrangles—Maps for America." http://nationalmap.gov/ustopo/index.html.

CHAPTER 3

COMPARING STANDARDS

Continuing, Different, and Added Practices

WHAT, AND HOW MUCH, IS GOING TO BE DIFFERENT FROM AACR2?
In the big picture of the move to RDA, the short answer to this question is, not a lot! This should provide at least a measure of relief, especially for catalogers, who, like the authors, have created bibliographic records using AACR2 for a number of years.

This chapter discusses on a broad level practices that remain the same in RDA as in AACR2, as well as specific differences between the two cataloging standards. Of course, learning the differences is critically important on this journey from the past and present into the future, and therefore attribute-level details about differences for variable fields will be discussed in chapter 4. To help, table 3.1 compares AACR2 rules with matching RDA instructions that are specific or common to cartographic resources.

In the first section, the authors will emphasize what remains the same, covering fixed-field coding and coded variable fields as well as the 1XX through 8XX MARC field areas. In addition, there is an overview of facsimile cartographic resources. The next section will introduce those differences between the standards that are either changes in practice or new applications of data.

Table 3.1
Comparison of RDA Instruction Number versus AACR2 Rule Number,
and their Location in MARC Fields*

Topic	MARC field/subfield	RDA instruction	AACR2 rule
Scale	255 $a	7.25	3.3B
Projection	255 $b	7.26	3.3C
Coordinates	255 $c	7.4.2	3.3D
Extent	300 $a	3.4.2	3.5B
Color	300 $b	7.17.1.3	3.5C5
Layout	300 $b	3.11	3.5C2
Polarity	300 $b	3.14	3.5C3
Mounting	300 $b	3.8	3.5C8
Production method	300 $b	3.9	3.5C3
Base materials	300 $b	3.6	3.5C6

*According to common cartographic resources descriptive elements.

OVERVIEW OF WHAT REMAINS THE SAME

Fixed Fields

From the Type of Record (Type) fixed field, which defines the record description as either a manuscript or non-manuscript cartographic item, all the way through the suite of fixed fields that apply to cartographic resources, the majority of coding practices in RDA remains the same as in AACR2. In fact, the single major change is not an addition or deletion of applicable fixed fields for describing cartographic resources, but a slight change in the code most commonly used in the Descriptive Cataloging Form (Desc) fixed field. Code "i," which stands for "ISBD" and is defined as the "descriptive portion of the record [that] contains the punctuation provisions of ISBD" in OCLC's *Bibliographic Formats and Standards*, will now be the de facto default code for those records that still use ISBD punctuation.

All other fixed fields—Bibliographic Level, Cartographic Type, Encoding Level, Form of Material, Index, Source, Government Publication, Projection, Relief, Special Form, Type of Date, Dates, Type of Control, Modified Record, Language, and Country of Publication—remain the same, and must be appropriately coded according to the resource being described and the elements contained within it.

Coded Variable Fields

This is another area that largely remains unchanged from AACR2 to RDA. There is only a slight change to the Cataloging Source field (MARC 040). The language of the catalog record is now explicitly given in $b using codes found in the MARC Code List for Languages (www.loc.gov/marc/languages/langhome.html); the descriptive standard used for cataloging—RDA in this case—is coded "rda" in $e. The order of subfields in OCLC is $a, $b, $e, and $c, where the institution's code for $c is system-supplied. For example:

    040   UPM $b eng $e rda $c UPM

The International Standard Book Number (020), Coded Cartographic Mathematical Data (034), Language Code (041), Geographic Area Code (043), Time Period of Content (045), Geographic Classification (052), and all the classification and call number fields remain unchanged.

1XX Fields

The 1XX field will still be a part of most cartographic resource records, although the authorized name of the entity is now called the "creator." Determining whether or not a corporate body can be considered a creator of a resource is guided by RDA 19.2.1, where 19.2.1.1.1 "f) cartographic works originating with a corporate body other than a body that is merely responsible for their publication or distribution" is worded similarly to the familiar text in AACR2 21.1B2.

The chief change that occurs here is in the names of these fields. As of the time of writing, the name of this section of the MARC 21 format is "Main Entry Fields." Because "main entry" is an AACR2 term not used in RDA, there is some expectation that the name will be changed to reflect the new circumstance. Additionally, some information has been added to this field, which is described later in the "Differences" section of this chapter.

245–246: Title and Varying Form of Title Field

In determining the title of a cartographic resource, "title" is a core element, and the resource in its entirety continues to determine the title. (The concept of "core" is discussed in detail in the "Differences" section, below.) If no subtitle is present, continue to supply one to indicate geographic area or topic covered by the resource, using 245$b, when this information is needed for clarity. RDA 2.3.4.5 thoroughly covers this situation.

25X–26X: Edition, Mathematical Data, and Imprint-Related Fields

Catalogers continue to record edition statements when they are present on the resource. A slight change from AACR2 is that edition statements are now transcribed as they appear, so there will be far fewer supplied abbreviations in this field, for instance, to the word "edition."

Scale is a core element and is still recorded as a representative fraction when a scale statement is present. A slight difference is that when scale is *calculated*, the scale statement will no longer be set off in square brackets. Additionally, "approximately" is to be spelled out when scale is calculated from a bar graph. Projection remains a recorded element (although when RDA was first released it was a transcribed element). However, because the term "projection" does not appear in RDA table B.7, do not abbreviate it while recording this statement.

Most imprint-related data elements are core, so that has not changed considerably. What *has* changed is the field in which the information is recorded, from the 260 field to the 264 field. Details on the structure and use of the new 264 field appear in chapter 4.

300: Physical Description Field

The method used to determine if a resource is a single map, a map set, an atlas, or other cartographic resource has not changed. Sharing information about other physical characteristics that should be recorded in the 300 field also has not changed and neither have the methods for measuring cartographic resources.

5XX: Note Fields

Different types of notes are provided as they were in AACR2. Common notes include the source of title note, orientation note, includes note (e.g., "Includes text and location map"), and "on verso" note. This is probably the part of the bibliographic record that has changed least.

6XX: Subject Fields

When originally conceptualized, RDA was to include sections on recording relationships between concepts, objects, events, and places. As of this writing, that section of RDA is not yet completed; therefore, until Section 10 is written, continue current subject analysis practices, and provide subject and form/genre headings as done under AACR2.

7XX: Added Creator/Contributor Fields

In RDA, catalogers have much more discretion as to what additional creators and contributors they add to the bibliographic record than they did under AACR2. Catalogers may, if desired, add the same number of creators/contributors as is done using AACR2, though they may also add more (or, if preferred, fewer) creators/contributors. As explained below in the "Differences" section, the "rule of three" as a controlling or limiting factor is gone.

4XX/8XX: Series Fields

Cartographic resources can be issued in series, and catalogers must determine if a series should be traced or not. Series elements are also considered core in RDA, and must be transcribed. Practices related to series between the standards are unchanged.

If a series should be traced, continue to use authorized forms of these titles to connect resources related by the series in which they are issued. The intellectual process catalogers go through to make these determinations has not changed. Information about series statements as an attribute of a manifestation is found at RDA 2.12.

Facsimiles

The treatment of cartographic-resources facsimiles remains the same in RDA. RDA 1.11 addresses cataloging facsimiles for all resources:

> When describing a facsimile or reproduction, record the data relating to the facsimile or reproduction in the appropriate element. Record any data relating to the original manifestation as an element of a related work or related manifestation, as applicable.

This is how cartographic facsimiles have been treated for decades, though it is a change for many other types of resources.

Details about the application of data elements for facsimiles and sharing bibliographically linked data are included in the "Notes" section of chapter 4.

INTRODUCTION TO DIFFERENCES

Catalogers with experience cataloging cartographic resources under AACR2 rules will find that the differences between applying those rules and applying RDA instructions are minimal, and can be mastered in a relatively short period of time. Beyond these principal changes, others are significant, but are not difficult to learn and apply. The following explores differences at a broad level. (Field-by-field changes will be discussed in a later chapter.)

Overview of Concepts

Behind the less dramatic changes are some underpinnings that provide the rationales for specific element-level changes. These are based, once again, on the central principle of RDA being a relationship-based standard with the goal of assisting users through the ideal of *find, identify, select,* and *obtain.* In addition, the models derive from FRBR, in particular the Group 1 set of entities: work, expression, manifestation, and item (as discussed in chapter 2). At the practitioner's level, it is necessary to learn and apply concepts that are record-wide in scope. These are:

- mode of issuance (RDA 1.1.3)
- sources of information (RDA 2.2)
- "take what you see" (RDA 1.7)
- core and "core if" elements (RDA 1.3)

MODE OF ISSUANCE

Although the label may sound strange, this RDA descriptor encompasses categories of resources used in AACR2. Defined as "a categorization reflecting whether a resource is issued in one or more parts, the way it is updated, and its intended termination" (RDA 2.13.1.1), there are four types of mode of issuance. These are single units, multipart monographs, serials, and integrating resources, which parallel the types outlined in AACR2 rule 1.0A2. These four modes have a direct bearing on subsequent instructions in RDA used for the description of cartographic (and other) resources.

SOURCES OF INFORMATION

In the format-based structure of AACR2, the rules for what to record as descriptive information directly—or indirectly, through the use of square brackets—are based on the foundational principles of chief sources of information and prescribed sources of information. For instance, the chief source of information to describe a monograph is the title page; if it is missing, the title page verso is often used as the "substitute" for the title page (see AACR2 rule 2.0B1). In comparison, the chief source of information for cartographic resources is the entire item itself, including all parts of it and/or some kind of associated container if necessary, followed by accompanying material (see rule 3.0B2). Each of these rules is clear: if the necessary information cannot be found in the chief source or the prescribed sources, employ a set of square brackets around the cataloger's supplied information to tell the reader that "this is not a part of the item I am describing, but is found somewhere else and given to you through another means." A look at RDA shows that this basic idea has not disappeared, but instead it has been relabeled and broadened.

RDA 2.2 explains the concept of source of information, which is all-encompassing. RDA 2.2.1 states, "Apply the instructions given under 2.2.2–2.2.4 when choosing a source of information. Apply for all elements covered in chapter 2 unless the instructions on sources of information for the element specify otherwise."

RDA chapter 2 identifies manifestations and items. RDA 2.2.2.1 then provides a set of general guidelines for application. The step-by-step process is:

- Take information from the resource itself, including either the storage medium or the physical housing, or from accompanying material.
- If the necessary information is not found on or at any of these locations, then turn to RDA 2.2.2.3.1, which instructs the cataloger to use either "a label bearing a title that is permanently printed on or affixed to the resource, excluding accompanying textual material or a container." For online resources, use "embedded metadata in textual form that contains a title (e.g., metadata embedded in an MPEG video file)," as per RDA 2.2.2.3.2.

The following looks at how the element "title" is derived using RDA instructions and guidelines.

RDA 2.3.1 addresses basic instructions for recording titles. It begins with a scope note at 2.3.1.1, followed by an instruction for sources of information at 2.3.1.2. This in turn contains nine sub-instructions that are specific to types of the element known as "title" (e.g., title proper, other title information, and parallel title). Each sub-instruction contains a reference to another specific RDA instruction; for example, the instruction for title proper directs the user to RDA 2.3.2.2, which instructs the cataloger to "take the title proper from the preferred source of information for the identification of the resource as specified under 2.2.2–2.2.3. If there is no title provided within the resource itself, take the title proper from one of the sources specified under 2.2.4. Make a note on the source of the title proper, if required" (see 2.17.2.3).

What is the "preferred source of information"? RDA 2.2.2.1 instructs the cataloger to select as the preferred source of information "*a source forming part of the resource itself* that is appropriate to: a) the type of description (see 2.1) and b) the presentation format of the resource (see 2.2.2.2–2.2.2.4)" (emphasis added). For cartographic resources, the "resource itself" is the map, globe, remote-sensing image, atlas, or similar, so this is not a change from AACR2. The change is in understanding the instructions and possibly navigating between instructions to apply them.

To summarize:

- Start with the preferred source as given in RDA 2.2.2.1.
- If the title proper is not found, turn to one of the other sources indicated.
- Finally, if it is necessary to use an alternate (or outside) source, also provide a source of title note (see RDA 2.17.2.3) just as was done when using AACR2.

"TAKE WHAT YOU SEE" OR
THE PRINCIPLE OF REPRESENTATION

RDA introduces the idea of placing exactly what the cataloger sees on the resource being described into the record, with few exceptions. This means moving away from the implied and indirect and toward the explicit to help patrons more easily understand what is being shared and to help enable computers to manipulate and interpret strings of characters more accurately.

RDA 0.4 addresses the "Objectives and Principles governing Resource Description and Access." RDA 0.4.3.4, on representation, further describes the idea of "take what you see." The first sentence in this instruction instructs the cataloger to take what you see … [as] "the data describing a resource should reflect the resource's representation of itself."

Oliver (2010, 62) explains the importance and impact of this principle in cataloging work:

> This principle has an impact on the context of many instructions. By closely following the principle of representation, the process of describing a resource is simplified because there are fewer exceptions. It also opens the door to the possibility of automated data capture and data reuse, and to streamlined workflows.

This principle is applied through the process of transcribing what is seen on the resource itself or other preferred sources of information, just as in AACR2, but with far fewer exceptions. This, in turn, leads to fewer uses of square brackets to represent the cataloger attempting to say "this data came from another source," nearly eliminating the use of abbreviations, and definitely removing the use of Latin abbreviations and phrases that catalogers understand, but most users do not. An example of an instruction telling us to transcribe data in a given element is:

2.3.1.4 Recording Titles
Transcribe a title as it appears on the source of information (see 1.7).

RDA 1.7 is the key instruction regarding transcription practices for all elements. Transcription is applied within individual instructions covering specific elements and sub-elements as noted by the general guidelines found at 1.7.1:

The instructions in chapters 2–4 specify transcription of certain elements as they appear on the source of information. When transcribing, apply the following general guidelines . . . When these guidelines refer to an appendix, apply the additional instructions in that appendix, as applicable to the element being transcribed.

The first half of the first sentence quoted above essentially means "if it says to transcribe something in one of the instructions found in chapters 2 through 4, then do it," or more succinctly, "take what you see." This means some titles might be transcribed *exactly* as found on the resource, including using all capital letters or capitalizing the first letter of each word. Although this is true to the principle, following the current practice of only capitalizing the first word and any proper name is recommended, particularly in the case of titles in which all letters are printed in upper case.

Remember also that in terms of abbreviations, if a word on the resource is found in its abbreviated form (or *an* abbreviated form, because many words can be abbreviated in different ways), then it is fine to put it in the bibliographic description in that manner (see appendix B.4 of RDA). This differs from AACR2, which allows the cataloger to abbreviate many words according to sets of tables, via specific rules, or even according to "past practice." In fact, this still occurs in RDA to a slight degree, through the use of four tables in appendix B. However, RDA B.4 is also clear about transcription and the application of abbreviations under specific circumstances: "For transcribed elements, use only those abbreviations found in the sources of information for the element. If supplying all or part of a transcribed element, generally do not abbreviate words."

The preceding sentence truly states the greatest difference between the standards: in general, do not abbreviate unless under very specific circumstances.

The following example of how the same data element is treated in AACR2 and RDA shows how "take what you see" is applied.

AACR2 Practice

> **3.3C** Statement of projection
>> **3.3C1.** Give the statement of projection if it is found on the item, its container or case, or accompanying printed material. Use abbreviations as instructed in Appendix B and numerals as instructed in Appendix C.
>> **EXAMPLE**
>> conic equidistant proj. ["projection" appears in AACR Appendix B.9 and therefore can be abbreviated in the record]

RDA Practice

> **7.26.1.3** Recording Projection of Cartographic Content
>> Record the projection of cartographic content if considered important for identification or selection.
>> **EXAMPLE**
>> conic equidistant projection ["projection" does *not* appear in RDA appendix B and therefore is not allowed to be abbreviated in the record]

A best practice for recording descriptive data for cartographic resources is never abbreviating a word unless it appears in that manner on the resource and the pertinent instruction also specifies transcribing the data. Indeed, RDA currently allows abbreviating under its appendix B guidelines, which will be covered below in the discussion of exceptions to abbreviating practices in RDA.

The authors agree with Oliver's contention that overall, the principle of "take what you see" does simplify the cataloging process because generally it is not necessary to know and apply exceptions to rules nor memorize specific words that can be abbreviated, nor look them up in a table to be certain. However, a major exception to this is related to geographic name abbreviation conventions through the use of RDA table B.11. Cataloger's judgment should be applied to abbreviating geographic names to help catalog users to understand a given abbreviated place name.

CORE ELEMENTS AND "CORE IF"

The notion of a "core record" has been around for some time, most noticeably as part of LC's cooperative cataloging efforts. One example of a formal core record standard can be found in the *BIBCO Standard Record (BSR) for Cartographic Materials Metadata Application Profile (MAP)*, which was implemented in 2010. Even outside of a formal situation such as this, "core" continues to mean "the minimum level of critical information that we can share with users so that they understand what this 'thing' is about." In other words, we must provide enough information to meet the functional objectives and principles as stated in RDA 1.2.

In the past, the level of the bibliographic *record* as a whole was considered when determining if something was core; however, RDA looks at another level of granularity, the *element*. This is understandable considering the context of the FRBR model and its use as the basis for identifying relationships within and between resources. It is at the level of elements that relationships work best and therefore support the FRBR and FRAD user tasks. Oliver notes that:

> RDA does not identify "levels" of description. It also does not identify each element as mandatory or optional. RDA takes a different approach and identifies a set of elements that are considered to be the minimum set. These elements are the ones that contain data about the attributes and relationships that have the highest value in fulfilling user tasks.

Which cartographic fields are core elements in RDA? Not surprisingly, they are the fields related to pieces of information that are most critical to the users of these records, such as title, creator, scale, and physical description. RDA 0.6.1 gives specific information about how the core elements are to be used, but also indicates the possible need to add more non-core elements to the description:

> As a minimum, a resource description for a work, expression, manifestation, or item should include all the core elements that are applicable and readily ascertainable. The description should also include any additional elements that are required in a particular case to differentiate the resource from one or more other resources with similar identifying information.

Be aware in the statement above of the latitude given to each situation, in particular "core elements that are applicable and readily ascertainable." Does this mean that catalogers can ignore the inclusion of something like a title if it is not a part of the resource? Definitely not, for RDA also offers the flexibility to seek out and use data taken from other areas beyond the resource in hand, just as AACR2 did. This simply means to pay attention to which elements are designated as core and make sure to act upon them.

Similar to the explicitly designated core elements are what have become known as "core if" elements. These are used in those instances where there is no access to data for a core element, and catalogers provide this data *if* they have access to the information, or employ an alternate type of data *if* they have exhausted the data types they are supposed to use, hence "core if" elements. An example of this is copyright date. Under the header for copyright date (RDA 2.11), which is a "core if" element, is this explicit statement: "Copyright date is a core element if neither the date of publication nor the date of distribution is identified." It turns out that because of the existing practice of providing a copyright date for cartographic resources as part of the MARC 260 subfield "c" for date of publication in AACR2, this is a change to which it will be relatively easy to adjust. Therefore, be on the lookout for similar "core if" statements like this that provide guidance in situations where data for a core element is lacking.

A list of core elements for attributes of manifestations and items that pertain to all resources can be found in RDA 0.6.2. Each of these elements, when present on the resource, must be a part of the bibliographic record. Note that many of these are designated "core if" due to a specific circumstance. (These will be discussed in detail in chapter 4, which focuses on field-level data.)

In addition to the core elements outlined in RDA 0.6.2, here are a few core/"core if" elements listed below specific to cartographic resources that do not appear in the list. Details on the application of these elements can be found in the next chapter.

Scale Statement (RDA 7.25)

Scale statements are core and include horizontal, vertical, angular, or other measurements. They also include the non-representative fraction (or non-numeric) statements:

- Scale not given
- Scales differ
- Scale varies
- Not drawn to scale

Projection (RDA 7.26)

Projection statements are considered core elements for LC catalogers and PCC participants, "core if" for everyone else (see LC-PCC PS 7.26).

Coordinates (RDA 7.4)

Including coordinate values in the record is core for LC catalogers and PCC participants, "core if" for everyone else (see LC-PCC PS 7.4.2 for guidance). Providing coordinates in the record at all times is strongly encouraged.

Digital File Characteristics (RDA 3.19)

As stated in the LC-PCC PS for RDA 3.19, "digital file characteristic is a core element for LC for cartographic resources." RDA 3.19.1.3 requires recording "digital file characteristics if considered important for identification or selection" and then provides a list of these types of characteristics, followed by the critical advice that when working with "digitally encoded cartographic content, also record data type, object type, and number of objects (see 3.19.8)." Providing this information whenever possible is recommended.

Layout (RDA 3.11)

Terms used to describe layout in the physical description, specifically "both sides" and "back to back," are core for cartographic resources (see the LC-PCC PS for the RDA 3.11 instruction on layout). Examples of the meaning and use of these terms are found at RDA 3.11.1.3.

Notes (RDA 2.17)

RDA highlights one type of note that applies to most resources, including cartographic. This note is commonly referred to as the source of title note—formally the note on title (RDA 2.17.2). Although not a part of the list of core elements in RDA 0.6.2, it is core for PCC and LC catalogers, as shared in LC-PCC PS 2.17.2. (See chapter 4 of this manual, which includes a detailed section on notes as they apply to cartographic resources.)

Overview of Continuing but Different Practices

ABBREVIATIONS AND ACRONYMS

In a desire to be more easily understood by users across the spectrum of delivery mechanisms (from the traditional online public access catalog, to today's discovery interfaces and social media and beyond), cataloger- or librarian-centric terminology in the form of abbreviations and acronyms is nearly eliminated in RDA. For instance, although catalogers all know that "ill." means either "illustration" or "illustrations" in our descriptions, perhaps some users have read this and wondered what it meant. Table 3.2 compares several words no longer abbreviated when using RDA.

A major, pertinent change for cartographic resources is that RDA does not use the familiar "ca." to stand in for "approximately" in scale statements. The spelled-out word is employed instead. This may seem odd the first few times it is used in a record,

Table 3.2
Commonly Abbreviated Words in AACR2 Compared to Transcribed Form in RDA

AACR2 abbreviation	RDA word usage
ill.	illustration; illustrations
ca.	approximately
col.	color
diam.	diameter
hand col.	hand colored
ms.	manuscript

and it does take a few more keystrokes to input, but as with other changed abbreviations it soon becomes familiar.

AACR2 EXAMPLE

255   Scale [ca. 1:100,000].

RDA EXAMPLE

255   Scale approximately 1:100,000.

AACR2 EXAMPLE

255   Scale ca. 1:250,000. [where "approximately" or its abbreviation "approx.," or another word meaning the same thing such as "about," appears this way on the resource]

RDA EXAMPLE

255   Scale approximately 1:250,000.

Exceptions to Abbreviating Practices in RDA

Just as with AACR2 and prior cataloging rules and standards, there are exceptions to the new abbreviating practices ushered in by RDA. These exceptions mean that a few abbreviation practices have not been changed although these could change in the future, as noted below.

A primary exception that still applies to cartographic resources is that abbreviating some units of measurement is permitted. RDA appendix B defines specific provisions for instances where transcribed words may be abbreviated, such as in RDA B.5 where each instruction includes "use symbols or abbreviations in the list at B.7." For instance, RDA B.5.1 states that when "recording dimensions (see 3.5), use symbols or abbreviations in the list at B.7 that apply to units of measurement. Metric symbols are not abbreviations and are not followed by a full stop." Checking the table in B.7 shows that it is acceptable to abbreviate "foot" or "feet" as "ft." and "inch" or "inches" as "in." A discussion about using metric dimensions such as centimeters and kilometers appears below.

Another primary exception is that RDA allows abbreviation of place names such as states and provinces in the United States and Canada, respectively. However, the authors learned that the British Library sent Proposal 6JSC/BL/10/BL (follow up) to the Joint Steering Committee for Development of RDA (JSC) at the time this book went to press. This proposal would remove the exception status for place names in resource descriptions, name headings, and access points; catalogers would no longer be allowed to abbreviate place names but instead would be required to apply the full geographic name.

Metric Terms Are Not Abbreviations

A unique change that applies to all resources but is more pronounced for catalogers of cartographic resources in the United States has to do with the shortened form of "centimeter" used for dimensions in MARC field 300$c. The metric linear measurement of centimeters has long been written in records as "cm.," with the period included, and in the United States at least has been thought of as an abbreviation. In fact, much of the rest of the world has used metric measurements for decades, but never considered the shortened form of centimeters (or other metric measurements, such as kilometers) to be an abbreviation but rather a *symbol*. Therefore, catalogers in the United States should be following the part of RDA B.5.1 related to metric terms, which states "metric symbols are not abbreviations." The following examples highlight this change:

AACR2

1 map : col. ; 25 x 35 cm.
1 map : col. ; 48 cm. in diam.
1 map on 2 sheets ; 95 x 65 cm., sheets 48 x 68 cm.
9 maps on 1 sheet : both sides, col. ; 19 x 10 cm. or smaller, sheet 26 x 33 cm.

RDA

1 map : color ; 25 x 35 cm
1 map : color ; 48 cm in diameter
1 map on 2 sheets ; 95 x 65 cm, sheets 48 x 68 cm
9 maps on 1 sheet : both sides, color ; 19 x 10 cm or smaller, sheet 26 x 33 cm

THE "RULE OF THREE" IS GONE

AACR2 used the generically coined "rule of three," which specifically applied to the Statement of Responsibility but also crept into other areas of the record based on practice and expediency. RDA eliminates this. This change has two aspects when dealing specifically with the Statement of Responsibility (MARC field 245$c): it is no longer acceptable to provide only the first three names of persons or corporate bodies in a statement of responsibility, and then to indicate this lack of additional information in the record via the use of "et al." as a supplied Latin phrase. These nuances will be explored further in chapter 4's discussion of statements of responsibility. We will also show how one can continue to share that multiple bodies were responsible for the creation of the resource but not explicitly stated in the record.

PRACTICE OF USING SQUARE BRACKETS TO SHOW CATALOGER-INTRODUCED DATA

When describing cartographic resources under AACR2, square brackets appear most prominently in scale information (MARC field 255$a), and also in information observed in the Publication, Distribution, Etc. area (MARC field 260, which will be covered in the discussion of the new 264 field in chapter 4). Although the practice has not been eliminated entirely in RDA, the use of square brackets has been relegated to more of an exception than the norm. The following section describes changes related to square brackets as a means of sharing information derived from sources other than the resource itself.

Application of Square Brackets in General

When is it acceptable to use square brackets in RDA? Generally speaking, the use of square brackets to indicate to the viewer of the record that a data element has been supplied by the cataloger is restricted more than in AACR2 because of changes to the former "rule of three," and an increase in the number of places from where the cataloger can derive information.

RDA 2.2.4 addresses other sources of information, a key provision related to describing a resource. It states:

> If information required to identify the resource does not appear on a source forming part of the resource itself (see 2.2.2.1), take it from one of the following sources (in order of preference):
>
> a) accompanying material (e.g., a leaflet, an "about" file) that is not treated as part of the resource itself as described in 2.2.2.1
>
> b) other published descriptions of the resource
>
> c) a container that is not issued with the resource itself (e.g., a box or case made by the owner)
>
> d) any other available source (e.g., a reference source).

However, if none of the above can be applied to the situation:

> When instructions specify transcription, indicate that the information is supplied from a source outside the resource itself:
>
> by means of a note (see 2.17)
>
> *or*
>
> by some other means (e.g., through coding *or the use of square brackets*) [emphasis added].

Those with experience cataloging cartographic resources, especially sheet maps, already know that this situation usually arises when at least one key element for a description is missing. Examples include a date or an indication of who was responsible for the map's creation, sometimes a scale, and occasionally a title. Now that more sources of information can be used to discover needed data, square brackets will be used less frequently.

To share an example, very often a map lacks a formal publication statement, in other words, something that explicitly tells the cataloger when and by whom it was published. A good example is the small United States Central Intelligence Agency map (see figure 2.1). They have been around since the 1950s, and at least sometimes showed the Agency's logo, information from which to infer the publisher's name. However, for decades they have been produced with absolutely no indication on the map of who the publisher is, where it is located, and a formal date on which the map was published (however, a printed alphanumeric code provides an inferred date of publication; see figure 2.3). A list of sources of information for publication statements is found at RDA 2.8.1.2, but because the resource itself lacks the needed data so that the publisher, place of publication, and date of publication must be supplied, the cataloger is told to go to RDA 2.2.4. Doing so locates the statement that when "instructions specify transcription, indicate that the information is supplied from a source outside the resource itself ... or by some other means (e.g., through coding *or the use of square brackets*)" (emphasis added).

In addition to using square brackets with supplied data such as for a place or date of publication, RDA 2.2.4 permits adding a note to the record to indicate the source of information employed for any element that is to be transcribed, including those of Title, Statement of Responsibility, Production/Publication/Manufacture/Distribution/Copyright, Edition, Serials Numbering, and Series. A common element that provides justification for data appearing in square brackets for cartographic resources is the source of title note. The note is given not only when a title is missing, which is fairly uncommon, but more often to identify the physical location from where the title was taken. Examples of common 500 note wording for source of title include "Title from panel," "Title from cover," "Title from envelope," "Panel title," and "Cover title." That said, it is also good practice to indicate where a source of information for any key data element has been derived (especially when it has been difficult to locate on the resource), or, more importantly, when it was supplied from a source outside of the resource itself, for example, from a website. Notes that justify key data elements at the very least help other catalogers in the identification process when looking for copy, and may also assist users.

Another place where square brackets are commonly used is the publication area. This will be covered briefly later in this chapter, and in depth as part of the 264 field in chapter 4.

Application of Square Brackets in Adjacent Elements

Another subtle but important change is how to apply square brackets to adjacent data elements in the new 264 field. Users of AACR2 were accustomed to placing square brackets around the entire 260 field, or sometimes placing them around two adjacent parts, such as place of publication and name of publisher. Although it is still acceptable to use square brackets to supply inferred information, including when no data are available, RDA specifies placing the brackets around each data element separately. RDA D.1.2.1 states that "when adjacent elements within one area are to be enclosed in square brackets, enclose each in its own set of square brackets."

AACR2 EXAMPLE

260   [Washington, D.C. : $b U.S. Bureau of the Census, $c 1970?]

RDA EXAMPLE

264 1   [Washington, D.C.] : $b [U.S. Bureau of the Census], $c [1970?]

OVERVIEW OF ADDED PRACTICES

As mentioned in the introduction to this chapter, some of the "differences" wrought by RDA have to do with including new fields of information, primarily the MARC 336 (content type), 337 (media type), and 338 (carrier type) fields, or new subfield-level information in the form of relationship designators (MARC subfield "e" for terms, or subfield "4" for codes as part of access points). Another new situation is the change from the former Publication, Distribution, Etc., Area in AACR2 in which the MARC 260 field was used. It has become the new MARC 264 field called Production, Publication, Distribution, Manufacture, and Copyright Notice.

33X Fields (Content Type, Media Type, Carrier Type)

To provide some context, recall that in AACR2 the General Material Designation, or GMD, found in 245$h is used to segregate formats of materials into categories using supplied labels such as "[microform]." Then, the Specific Material Designation, or SMD, in MARC field 300$a provided more specificity. In RDA, the idea of sharing what type of resource is being described has been broken out into three new fields and the GMD is eliminated. This was done both to provide better levels of specificity and to enhance resource descriptions for use in linked data and other content schemas. Note that these fields are repeatable in order to accommodate a resource with multiple characteristics, and the terms that are used in the "types" in subfield "a" come from a controlled vocabulary.

These fields are:

- the MARC 336 field for content type, for which instructions are found in RDA 6.9
- the MARC 337 field for media type, for which instructions are found in RDA 3.2

- the MARC 338 field for carrier type, for which instructions are found in RDA 3.3

This is in keeping with one of the underlying "key features" of RDA. As stated in RDA 0.1:

> RDA provides a flexible and extensible framework for the description of resources produced and disseminated using digital technologies while also serving the needs of agencies organizing resources produced in non-digital formats. RDA is designed to take advantage of the efficiencies and flexibility in data capture, storage, retrieval, and display made possible with new database technologies.

A more complete explanation of each field and its contents, with examples for most types of cartographic resources, is found in chapter 4. The document "RDA in MARC" (www.loc.gov/marc/RDAinMARC.html) contains bulleted key points and links to the tables showing all 33X terms and codes involved. In addition, appendix E of this manual contains a document titled "33X Content, Media, and Carrier Terms Examples based on Different Kinds of Cartographic Resources," which consists of sets of 33X fields according to the specific type of resource being described. The authors hope that this visual representation will be of great assistance to catalogers learning to construct these new fields.

RELATIONSHIP DESIGNATORS

Relationship designators (RDs) have been around for some time, and are used more frequently in records for some types of resources—such as music—than others. Therefore, it is safe to say that for cartographic resources catalogers this constitutes a new practice.

Information about the use of relationship designators is found in RDA appendixes I, J, K, and L. The authors recommend reviewing the scope statements at the beginning of each appendix for guidance on how and when to use the terms. Each appendix covers a different set of relationships, as follows:

APPENDIX I: relationships between a resource and the persons, families, and corporate bodies associated with it

APPENDIX J: relationships between work, expression, manifestation, and item

APPENDIX K: relationships between persons, families, and corporate bodies

APPENDIX L: relationships between concepts, objects, events, and places (forthcoming)

A table containing a non-comprehensive list of relationship designators that we typically see associated with creators and contributors of cartographic resources, as found in appendix I, follows.

Creators	Contributors
cartographer	cartographer (expression)
compiler	platemaker
creator	surveyor
issuing body	engraver
sponsoring body	lithographer

Additionally, sometimes these terms are found as part of a statement of responsibility, though not necessarily in their standardized forms as shown above. The key difference between a similar or same designator (or role) term as found in 245$c and those found elsewhere are that they are applied with an authorized access point in a $e, as shown in these examples:

100 1   Raisz, Erwin, $d 1893-1968, $e cartographer.
110 2   Geological Survey (U.S.), $e cartographer.
110 2   O.H. Bailey & Co., $e creator, $e lithographer.
710 2   American Red Cross, $e issuing body.

Must catalogers provide these designators in their descriptions? The short answer is no (though this may change in the future). However, catalogers at institutions that are members of the Monographic Bibliographic Record Program (BIBCO) of the Program for Cooperative Cataloging at the Library of Congress must follow a set of PCC guidelines for applying relationship designators. The PCC Guidelines for the Application of Relationship Designators in Bibliographic Records (www.loc.gov/aba/pcc/rda/PCC%20RDA%20guidelines/Relat-Desig-Guidelines.docx) advises including "a relationship designator for all creators, whether they are coded MARC 1XX or MARC 7XX. If the MARC 1XX is not a creator, the addition of a relationship designator is optional though strongly encouraged. Add a relationship designator even if the MARC field definition already implies a relationship." Then, under a following list of guidelines, Guideline 2 also recommends "that PCC catalogers use relationship designators from the RDA appendices," and if one is not listed there to "use the PCC relationship designator proposal form to propose a new term or request a revision of an existing term." Finally, even if an institution is not a BIBCO member, the PCC Guidelines provide assistance to several relationship designators (RDs) questions and could prove to be useful in local situations.

Two particular RD terms that were initially forbidden for use in the bibliographic record because they also are RDA Toolkit element names are "creator" and "publisher." However, Guideline 4 of the PCC Guidelines signals a change of course, stating:

Assign an RDA element name as a relationship designator, e.g., "creator" (19.2) or "publisher" (21.3) if it will most appropriately express the relationship. Note: This

departure from RDA is necessary in our current MARC environment to express
the relationship because not all RDA elements have dedicated MARC fields.

But it also asks that no terms that are also RDA element names be proposed. For
cartographic resources, the ability to include these two terms greatly enhances the
specificity of the role of a given person or corporate body noted in the records.

How relationship designators (or codes) should be handled is certain to be a part
of each of the "best practices" documents being formulated by many cataloging
communities.

264 Field (Production, Publication, Distribution, Manufacture, and Copyright Notice)

The differences between the "old" AACR2-specific 260 field and the new RDA-specific
264 field are substantial. In the past, all elements related to publication, production,
and similar data generally were placed within a single 260 field that used numerous
subfields to specify the kind of activity involved. With the emergence of the repeatable 264 field, these activities are now separated by role, placing each type in its own
field and identifying the role through a specific second Indicator value. By doing
so, the data are more "flexible and extensible" (as noted in RDA 0.1 above); in other
words, it is easier to manipulate specific data element types by computer under this
new structure.

Fortunately, the details, definitions, and explanations of how this new 264 field
is used are clearly outlined in LC's *MARC 21 Format for Bibliographic Data*. There
are also other guidelines for catalogers, including the "PCC Guidelines for the 264
Field," which is a Microsoft Word document that can be found online (www.loc.gov/
aba/pcc/documents/264-Guidelines.doc). The authors use the MARC bibliographic
record standard as the reader's primary guide, and share instructions and some
cartographic-specific examples of this new field in chapter 4.

Indeed, there *are* differences between AACR2 rules and RDA instructions when
it comes to describing cartographic resources! Those differences fall into a couple of
categories: ones that catalogers have followed in practice for decades, but which differ
in scope and application, and to a lesser degree, those that can be considered brand
new. For clarification, see appendix C of this book, which is a checklist of many of the
changes discussed above.

Chapter 4 covers field-by-field navigation and application of RDA instructions
related to cartographic resources; in reality, however, many of these apply to all kinds
of resources. The authors hope that this chapter has reassured readers that the leap
from the familiar land of AACR2 to the unknown or lesser-known land of RDA truly
is not that great.

REFERENCES

Joint Steering Committee for the Development of RDA. "Revision of 9.8.1.3, 9.9.1.3, 9.10.1.3, 9.11.1.3, 10.5.1.3, 11.3.1.3, 11.13.1.3, 16.2.2.4, 16.2.2.9.2, B.1, B.11 to eliminate use of abbreviations for places. British Library Follow up." February 21, 2014. www.rda-jsc.org/docs/6JSC-BL-10-BL-follow-up.pdf.

Library of Congress. Network Development and MARC Standards Office. MARC 21 Bibliographic Format. 264—Production, Publication, Distribution, Manufacture, and Copyright Notice. www.loc.gov/marc/bibliographic/bd264.html.

———. MARC Code List for Languages. www.loc.gov/marc/languages/langhome.html.

———. RDA in MARC. www.loc.gov/marc/RDAinMARC.html.

Library of Congress. Program for Cooperative Cataloging. PCC Guidelines for the 264 Field. www.loc.gov/aba/pcc/documents/264-Guidelines.doc.

———. PCC Guidelines for the Application of Relationship Designators in Bibliographic Records. www.loc.gov/aba/pcc/rda/PCC%20RDA%20guidelines/Relat-Desig-Guidelines.docx.

Library of Congress. Program for Cooperative Cataloging. Monographic Bibliographic Record Program (BIBCO). www.loc.gov/aba/pcc/bibco/index.html.

———. BIBCO Core Record Standards (superseded by the BIBCO Standard Record Oct. 1, 2010). www.loc.gov/aba/pcc/bibco/coreintro.html. The Core Records Standard for Cartographic Materials is at www.loc.gov/aba/pcc/bibco/coremaps.html. The Bibliographic Standard Record Metadata Application Profile for cartographic materials is at www.loc.gov/aba/pcc/bibco/documents/BSR_CART_3Sept-2010.pdf.

Oliver, Chris. 2010. *Introducing RDA: A Guide to the Basics.* Chicago: American Library Association.

NAVIGATING RDA TO DESCRIBE CARTOGRAPHIC RESOURCE ELEMENTS

THIS CHAPTER PRESENTS DETAILED INFORMATION THAT CAN BE considered the heart of the manual. It compares MARC fields describing cartographic resources to the RDA in structions that provide the guidelines for what and how to record descriptive element information. Where RDA is silent on certain points, the authors will refer to LC-PCC PSs and best practices.

245 FIELD: TITLE AND OTHER STATEMENTS

Although the MARC 245 field contains twelve subfields, this section is concerned with the four that are most commonly used. Of note, since implementation of RDA, subfield "h," which was used in AACR2 for the general material designation term or phrase, is no longer used. The three new 33X fields added to the MARC 21 format to replace the general material designation will be examined later in this chapter.

Background to Title and Other Statements

- Title proper is a core element.
- Remainder of title/other title information is "core if" (described below)

- Statement of responsibility is core.

The four data elements that will be covered here are the title proper in $a, title of part/section of a work in $p, other title information in $b, and the statement of responsibility in $c.

The most commonly used subfields are discussed below in the order that they usually appear in the bibliographic record. Examples use ISBD punctuation within the fields, although RDA does not require ISBD to be used. This is a standard practice for LC and PCC catalogers, and it is assumed that most institutions will follow this practice.

245$a TITLE PROPER

Building on the discussion in chapter 3 that explained that the title is a transcribed element in RDA, a title is defined as "a word, character, or group of words and/or characters that names a resource or a work contained in it"(2.3.1.1.). Because the title of a resource can appear in different forms in or on the resource, RDA provides guidance in selecting the title proper (RDA 2.3.2), which may also refer the cataloger to the discussion of other resources at RDA 2.2.2.4. When dealing with a single map, the preferred source for title is a textual source on the resource itself or a label permanently printed or applied to the resource.

EXAMPLE

245 10 Water-level altitudes 2013, and water-level changes in the Chicot, Evangeline, and Jasper aquifers and compaction 1973-2012 in the Chicot and Evangeline aquifers, Houston-Galveston Region, Texas.

If there is no title on the resource, then take the title proper from a container or accompanying material. If the title proper is taken from anywhere other than the resource itself, the title is placed in brackets and a note provided to explain where the title came from. There is an option not to record the note; however, the LC-PCC PS says not to omit the note.

EXAMPLE

245 00 [Alabama outline map showing county boundaries]
500   Title from accompanying text.

If there is no title on the resource and no other source for a title, one is created by the cataloger according to the instruction for recording devised titles (RDA 2.3.2.11). This instruction provides three options for content of a created title: include the nature of the resource, its subject, or both; for cartographic resources, continue to follow the third option to include both the geographic area shown and subject of the resource whenever possible, but at minimum *always* include the geographic area.

EXAMPLE

245 10 [Map of Israel]
500   Title devised by cataloger.

Finally, if scale is stated as part of the title, include it in the title (RDA 2.3.2.8.2).

EXAMPLE

245 10 National topographic maps 1:250,000-scale series

If there is an error in the title (most commonly a typographic error), transcribe the title exactly as it appears on the resource. An added title with the title shown in its correct form, using the MARC 246 field, should then be included. Do not use the [i.e. …] convention used in AACR2 cataloging.

EXAMPLE

245 10 Raod map of Arizona
246 3 $i Corrected title: $a Road map of Arizona

There will be times when parts of the title are scattered over a map or there are several location-based options in choosing the title proper (see figure 4.1). The current best practice is to take the title that presents the fullest amount of information, no matter its location, as the title proper. It is also necessary to take into account the publishers' intent, if one can be discerned. For example, if a map is folded with either a panel or cover title, the publisher intends for the title on the panel or cover to be seen first. This should be the title proper chosen for the bibliographic record.

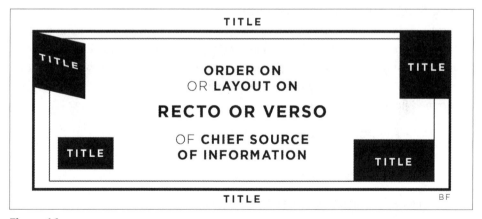

Figure 4.1
Choice of title proper in map layout

245$p TITLE OF PART OR SECTION OF A WORK

Of the four subfields discussed here, subfield "p" is the least used in cartographic resource cataloging. This subfield is often used when cataloging a map that could be considered part of a series but the decision has been made to use the series title as the title proper for all of the maps included.

EXAMPLE

245 10 Nelles maps. $p Northern India

This same methodology can be employed with a map set in which each map within the set is about a different topic but the choice has been made to catalog each map separately.

245$b OTHER TITLE INFORMATION

The general guideline for other title information is to record information that appears on the same source of information as the title proper (RDA 2.3.4.3). However, there is a special guideline for other title information for cartographic resources at RDA 2.3.4.5, which states that if the title proper does not include an indication of the geographic area covered and/or the subject portrayed, and the other title information also does not convey this or there is no other title information, then the cataloger should supply a brief phrase in square brackets indicating the geographic area and, if appropriate, the subject portrayed.

EXAMPLE

245 10 National topographic maps 1:250,000-scale series : $b [United States]

245$c STATEMENT OF RESPONSIBILITY

The statement of responsibility is defined as "a statement relating to the identification and/or function of any persons, families, or corporate bodies responsible for the creation of, or contributing to the realization of, the intellectual or artistic content of a resource" (RDA 2.4.1.1). As with the title proper, the statement of responsibility is a transcribed field (RDA 2.4.1.4).

EXAMPLE (SINGLE STATEMENT OF RESPONSIBILITY)

245 10 National topographic maps 1:250,000-scale series : $b [United States] / $c U.S. Geological Survey.

EXAMPLE (MULTIPLE STATEMENTS OF RESPONSIBILITY)

245 10 Water-level altitudes 2013, and water-level changes in the Chicot, Evangeline, and Jasper aquifers and compaction 1973-2012 in the Chicot and Evangeline aquifers, Houston-Galveston Region, Texas / $c by Mark C. Kasmarek, Michaela R. Johnson, and Jason K. Ramage ; prepared in cooperation with the

Harris-Galveston Subsidence District, City of Houston, Fort Bend Subsidence District, Lone Star Conservation District, and Brazoria County Groundwater Conservation District.

Additionally, if the statement of responsibility is named as part of the title, then it is not necessary to give the name in the 245$c. This is addressed in RDA 2.3.1.5: *if the title includes a name that would normally be treated either as part of a statement of responsibility or as the name of a publisher, distributor, etc., and the name is an integral part of the title (e.g., connected by a case ending), then record the name as part of the title.

EXAMPLE

110 2   Hagstrom Map Company.
245 10 Hagstrom New York City 5 borough large type 2009 street atlas.

Finally, as stated in the previous chapter, the "rule of three" used in AACR2 is gone. Although continuing to abridge the statement of responsibility when more than one person is named is an option at RDA 2.4.1.5, when "more than three persons, families, or corporate bodies" perform the same function, the LC policy is "generally do not omit names in a statement of responsibility." However, if the cataloger prefers to truncate a single statement of responsibility then the first named creator is given followed by "[and X others]" where X is the number of other creators not named, as noted by the optional omission in this instruction.

EXAMPLE (OPTIONAL OMISSION)

245 10 Water-level altitudes 2013, and water-level changes in the Chicot, Evangeline, and Jasper aquifers and compaction 1973-2012 in the Chicot and Evangeline aquifers, Houston-Galveston Region, Texas / $c by Mark C. Kasmarek, Michaela R. Johnson, and Jason K. Ramage ; prepared in cooperation with the Harris-Galveston Subsidence District, City of Houston, [and 3 others].

Although LC's Geography and Map Division is following the LC policy noted above and recording all creators in the statement of responsibility, cataloger's judgment will determine how many creators and contributors are named, as long as the cataloger follows the application of core elements.

250 FIELD: EDITION STATEMENTS

- Edition statements and named revisions of editions statements are core in RDA.

RDA 2.5 specifically says "designation of edition and designation of a named revision of an edition are core elements. Other sub-elements of edition statements are optional." The two instances where edition is considered a core element are covered by RDA 2.5.2 and 2.5.6, but another somewhat common situation with cartographic resources—when a statement of responsibility appears with the edition statement—is addressed by RDA 2.5.4.

- Edition statements are to be transcribed from the resource (RDA 2.5.1.4).

Cartographic resources, like many other resources, can be issued in editions and therefore fall under the definition in RDA 2.5.1.1, "a statement identifying the edition to which a resource belongs." However, this definition includes a key statement that applies frequently to cartographic resources: "An edition statement sometimes includes a designation of a named revision of an edition." Edition revision statements are relatively common with cartographic resources and are important because they indicate that some portion of the cartographic resource has been changed from a previous edition (e.g., the expansion of parts of a road network or the change of a political boundary). The statements indicating a revision as found on the resource may be as simple as "Revised [date]" or as complex as a full explanatory sentence.

As noted above, for some types of maps a statement of responsibility for the edition or the revision of an edition is given. In such circumstances the edition's statement of responsibility is placed in $b of the MARC 250 field, separated from the $a by a forward slash (called a "diagonal slash" in RDA appendix D), as denoted in RDA D.1.2.3. Examples are shown below with the discussion of RDA 2.5.4.

Sources of information for edition statements vary because of how a given edition statement may relate to different parts of the resource. There are eight scenarios presented in RDA (for specifics on all of them, see RDA 2.5.1.2). However, those that most frequently apply to cartographic resources are:

a) For designation of edition, see 2.5.2.2. …
c) For statement of responsibility relating to the edition, see 2.5.4.2. …
e) For designation of a named revision of an edition, see 2.5.6.2. …
g) For statement of responsibility relating to a named revision of an edition, see 2.5.8.2.

2.5.2 Designation of Edition

A designation of edition is a word, character, or group of words and/or characters, identifying the edition to which a resource belongs. Note that in some languages the same term or terms can be used to indicate both edition and printing. A statement detailing the number of copies printed is not a designation of edition. In case of doubt about whether a statement is a designation of edition, consider the presence of these words or statements as evidence that it is a designation of edition:

a) a word such as *edition, issue, release, level, state,* or *update* (or its equivalent in another language)

or

b) a statement indicating:

     i) a difference in content

     ii) a difference in geographic coverage

     iii) a difference in language

     iv) a difference in audience

     v) a particular format or physical presentation

     vi) a different date associated with the content

     vii) a particular voice range or format for notated music.

Common words designating editions for cartographic resources include "edition" (as well as a foreign language form such as "Auflage," "edición," or "edizione"), "preliminary edition," "revision" or "revised," "updated," and "corrected."

2.5.2.2 Sources of Information for Designations of Edition

Take designations of edition from the following sources (in order of preference):

a) the same source as the title proper (see 2.3.2.2)

b) another source within the resource itself (see 2.2.2)

c) one of the other sources of information specified at 2.2.4.

In situation (a), the majority of the time for cartographic resources the title proper and its source are one and the same, that is, the title proper appears anywhere as part of the map, globe, or similar. For sheet maps this means that the title might be found anywhere on the sheet(s), including either side. Thus, a designated edition most often falls within the first circumstance noted above.

Less common is situation (b), though when it does occur it means that the designated edition statement is located on something like the envelope in which a map was issued, perhaps an accompanying textual index of some kind, or even a separate title sheet for a map set or unbound atlas, rather than appearing as part of the cartographic resource.

The last instance, (c), is very unusual, but could be applied to early cartographic resources, particularly through the means of a cartobibliography serving as an "other published description of the resource," as described in RDA 2.2.4.

The examples of designations of edition shown below follow RDA instructions concerning abbreviating words; in all cases the examples show that the form of wording from the resource might either be abbreviated or spelled out; follow "take what you see" in either case.

250	2nd ed. (or 2nd edition or Second edition)
250	Edition of 1946 (or Ed. of 1946)
250	2010 ed. (or 2010 edition)
250	Edition 1
250	1998-99 ed. (or 1998-99 edition, or 1998-1999 edition)
250	Edición 1967
250	6. Aufl. (or 6. Auflage)

2.5.4 Statement of Responsibility Relating to the Edition

This is defined under RDA 2.5.4.1 as "a statement relating to the identification of any persons, families, or corporate bodies responsible for the edition being described but not to all editions." In addition, this is one of the "other sub-elements of edition statements" that is not core according to the core statement found at 2.5. It is included here because it is a common circumstance for cartographic resources, and the authors recommend that these statements be included in the description.

SOURCE OF INFORMATION FOR STATEMENT OF RESPONSIBILITY RELATING TO THE EDITION

RDA 2.5.4.2 instructs the cataloger to take such a statement of responsibility from the same source as that of the designation of the edition; most often these kinds of statement of responsibility for cartographic resources appear with or as part of the designation of edition.

As noted at the beginning of this section on edition statements, when a statement of responsibility associated with an edition is discovered it is placed in $b of the MARC 250 field, separated from $a by a forward slash. For instance:

250	5th ed. / $b edited by Richard Overy.
250	Actualisation partielle / $b Samantha Rekk.

2.5.6 Designation of a Named Revision of an Edition

This is the second core element for editions, defined in RDA 2.5.6.1 as "a word, character, or group of words and/or characters, identifying a particular revision of a named edition." RDA 2.5.6.2 also notes that sources of information for this element include:

a) the same source as the designation of edition (see 2.5.2.2)

b) another source within the resource itself (see 2.2.2)

c) one of the other sources of information specified at 2.2.4

RDA 2.5.6.3 specifies how to record this information: "If the source of information has a statement indicating a revision of an edition (e.g., a named reissue of a particular edition containing changes from that edition), record that statement. Apply the instructions on recording designations of edition (see 2.5.2.3)." An example might be the phrase "Roads revised" appearing as a statement in the cartographic resource, which also notes that it is the 4th edition of that resource. Therefore, it would appear as:

250   4th ed., roads revised. [form of "ed." appears this way in the resource]

Another important point specific to reissues of a given resource is raised in this instruction: "Do not record statements relating to a reissue of an edition that contains no changes unless the resource is considered to be of particular importance to the agency preparing the description." Although this is an uncommon occurrence for cartographic resources, it is worth noting for whenever it does arise.

255 FIELD: CARTOGRAPHIC MATHEMATICAL DATA (SCALE, PROJECTION, AND COORDINATES)

Note that although the MARC 255 field contains nine subfields, this section is concerned with the first three that are the most commonly encountered and necessary, as provided below. Those RDA instructions regarding statements of coordinate rings or pairs in $f and $g (RDA 7.4.3), statement of zone(s) or $d (RDA 7.4.4), and statement of equinox or $e (RDA 7.5) can be interpreted on one's own.

Background to Cartographic Mathematical Data

- Scale is a core element.
- Projection is "core if" (see the LC-PCC PS for instruction RDA 7.26).
- Coordinates are "core if" (see the LC-PCC PS for instructions RDA 7.4 and 7.4.2).

Three data elements that appear regularly in the MARC 255 field in records are the scale statement in $a, the projection statement in $b, and coordinate values in $c. The arrangement of the following text takes its cue from this set of elements. The following discussion treats the RDA instructions for the scale statement data elements first (projection statement and coordinate values are discussed later).

The two RDA instructions that apply to horizontal scale for cartographic resources are: basic instructions for recording scale (RDA 7.25.1) and horizontal scale of cartographic content (7.25.3). For instructions on recording vertical scale information, such as might be found with a geologic profile map, see RDA 7.25.4.

Instructions on dealing with cartographic projection statements are found in RDA 7.26, and instructions on coordinates of latitude and longitude and how to record them are found in RDA 7.4.

The good news regarding input of data into the MARC 255 field is that the necessary data and techniques are applied almost exactly as under AACR2. The methods for determining scale information and representing it in the record, handling "additional scale information," dealing with projection statements, and recording coordinates values are not changed substantially with the introduction of RDA. Those changes that did occur relate primarily to abbreviation practices, and also with the supplied word "Scale."

Determining the Scale when Present on the Resource or Elsewhere

255$a SCALE STATEMENT

Data in the 255$a may appear on the resource or its accompanying material in a form different than what the instructions specify *or* may not appear anywhere, in which cases the cataloger can use one of several methods to supply specific descriptive phrases. The key RDA instruction relating to the data that must appear in this area is in RDA 7.25.1.3, which specifies recording "the scale of the resource as a representative fraction expressed as a ratio." The instruction then is broken into several sub-instructions to describe what to do under specific circumstances. This parallels AACR2 rule 3.3B1.

When present on the resource or any source related to it, scale may be shown in one of three ways:

- as a representative fraction (RF)
- as a verbal scale, such as "1 inch to 4 miles"
- as a bar or "graph" that is segmented according to specific linear measurement types such as feet, miles, or kilometers

As noted in RDA 7.25.1.3, when describing a map with scale already stated in representative fraction form, it is simply a matter of recording it. And if the scale is stated as part of the title instead of in a location by itself, it is fine to take it from that location: "Record the scale even if it is already recorded as part of the title proper or other title information."

If, however, a scale statement on the resource appears in one of the other two methods noted above then there is more work to do:

> If the scale statement that appears in the resource is not expressed as a representative fraction, convert the scale statement into a representative fraction. … If no scale statement is found in the resource, take a scale statement from a source outside the resource. If this scale statement is not expressed as a representative fraction, convert the scale statement into a representative fraction.

Verbal Scale Statements

The most common units of measurement used for resources in the United States are inches, feet, yards, and miles (and many variant forms of "mile" such as Spanish mile or nautical mile), each of which can be converted mathematically to derive the RF. These all fall under the banner of Imperial units of linear measurements. For the rest of world the metric system rules and the common units on maps and other cartographic resources in this system are centimeters, meters, and kilometers. Again, each of these can be converted for the intended use. For example, consider the most common Imperial unit for maps, miles. Miles are used as a linear distance when a map depicts a large or relatively large geographic area such as those for a vast region (e.g., Yellowstone National Park in the United States or the Ural Mountains of the Soviet Union), or a state or similar administrative area (e.g., a Province in Canada or Argentina, Department in France or Division in Germany).

A mile is equivalent to 63,360 inches, so it is easy to take a verbal statement such as "1 inch equals 4 miles" and convert it to a RF. Simply multiply 63,360 by 4, which totals 253,440. Thus, the RF that appears in the record would be:

> 255   Scale 1:253,440

What do we do with the actual verbal statement? Refer to the section on additional scale information (RDA 7.25.5) where instruction 7.25.5.3 tells the cataloger to "record additional scale information that appears on the resource. Capitalize words as instructed in appendix A. Use abbreviations or symbols for units of measurement as instructed in appendix B (B.5.7) and numerals in place of words (see 1.8.3)." Thus, following the primary instruction of recording the scale statement as a representative fraction, the example above would be:

> 255   Scale 1:253,440. 1 in. equals 4 miles (abbreviating "inch" or "inches" is allowed in appendix B at table B.7)

Here is another example, this time dealing with a much smaller geographic area, and thus using the linear measurement of feet. A bathymetric fishing map of

Beltzville Lake in Pennsylvania states its scale as being "1″ = 667 feet." There are 12 inches in a foot, thus the calculation to convert this to a representative fraction would be 12 × 667 or 8004, which when recorded according to RDA instructions would be:

255   Scale 1:8,004. 1″ = 667 ft. (again, "feet" or "foot" appears in table B.7 and thus "feet" can be abbreviated)

All manner of verbal scales can be converted into RFs in this way. To do so, it is necessary to know the equivalent unit of measurement. This kind of information can be found online by searching something like "linear conversion calculator" and then letting the calculator do its work. Another valuable resource is appendix B of the manual *Cartographic Materials*, "Guidelines to Determine Scale and Coordinates."

What is the appropriate way to record a verbal scale statement? In AACR2, rule 3.3B1 required us to use square brackets under this circumstance, "If a scale statement found in the chief source of information or accompanying material is not expressed as a representative fraction, give it as a representative fraction in square brackets." There is no equivalent in RDA 7.25.1.3, which simply tells us to do the conversion. Therefore, in applying RDA do not use square brackets, even with a supplied data element, which is also shown correctly in the examples above. Note however that institutions may have recorded the denominator value of the RF in a different manner according to set practices, without a comma but with a space, and therefore may appear on copy such as:

255   Scale 1:63 360

Bar/Graphic Scales and How to Derive a Representative Fraction

Now to the question of how to handle the *approximate* ratio for a cartographic resource that only shows scale through the means of a bar (or sometimes called a "graphic") scale. After all, what appears on the resource would look something like what is shown in figure 4.2.

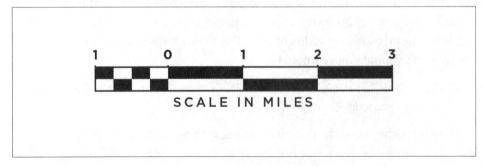

Figure 4.2
Illustration of a bar scale

Bar scales appear in many different formats, sometimes also including a representative fraction. One example of this situation is shown in figure 4.3.

This illustration shows the combination of multiple bar scales and additionally the representative fraction. In such cases, because the RF is already provided it should be used as the scale statement in the 255 field; there is no need to convert one of the bar scales to a representative fraction. But when all that is given is a bar scale similar to that shown in figure 4.2, how is the resulting RF recorded?

One part of RDA 7.25.1.3 says that "if no scale statement is found in the resource or in another source, estimate a representative fraction from a bar scale or a grid. Record *approximately* preceding the estimated representative fraction." This is a very important point: the abbreviation "ca." is no longer used, as was required in AACR2 rule 3.3.B1; instead, the actual word "approximately" is used. As a reminder, the next step in AACR2 rule 3.3B1 also required using square brackets in this circumstance. Once again, in using RDA *do not* use square brackets with this data element in this situation.

Going back to the original question of how to get from a graphic bar representing scale to an actual numeric ratio, the answer is "with a tool that does the measuring for you." Although the RF can be derived in this circumstance using a common ruler, the best tool for this job is known as a Natural Scale Indicator, or sometimes a Map Scale Indicator. To acquire a Natural Scale Indicator, consult the Map Librarian's Toolbox (www.waml.org/maptools.html) at the Western Association of Map Libraries' website (or other similar toolboxes on the Internet). To learn how to use this remarkable tool, refer to the YouTube video at www.youtube.com/watch?v=vSus_5bt440.

After doing the work to determine the RF, the RDA instructions are clear; use the word "approximately" in front of the ratio. This word must be applied to tell users that the figure was determined from a tool, rather than taken directly from the map, and because the accuracy of eyesight varies from person to person the result is an approximation, whereas when doing a mathematical calculation with a verbal statement it is not. The example shown in RDA is:

approximately 1:1,200

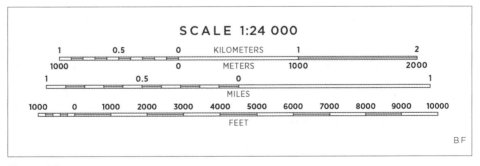

Figure 4.3
Examples of different bar scales view

However, by following the best practice of adding the word "Scale" to this statement to make it more understandable, as noted below, the scale statement would appear in the record as:

255   Scale approximately 1:1,200

Supplying the Word "Scale" to Begin the Scale Statement

In AACR2 the very first rule in 3.3B states:

> **3.3B1.** Give the scale of a cartographic item (except as noted below) as a representative fraction expressed as a ratio (1:). Precede the ratio by *Scale*. Give the scale even if it is already recorded as part of the title proper or other title information.

The shortest sentence in the AACR2 rule above tells the cataloger *to supply* the word "Scale" to begin the scale statement itself. This is true for the situation in which a scale of some kind is explicitly present on the resource; however, in the very specific circumstances described below it will be necessary instead to supply one of four long-established phrases to tell users what is going on (these are "Scale not given," "Scales differ," "Scale varies," and "Not drawn to scale").

The notable change in RDA is that the scale statement that appears in 255$a is *not* a transcribed element because the data are supplied through one of several means, though the most straightforward of these means is by "transcribing" or lifting a representative fraction as it is found on the resource. Therefore, there is no instruction for adding the word "Scale" in front of the representative fraction. In fact, catalogers in other areas of the world have never supplied the word "Scale," and likely will continue to follow that practice. If RDA 7.25.1.3 is interpreted literally, what appears in 255$a is simply the RF as found or as determined by the cataloger, "record the scale of the resource as a representative fraction expressed as a ratio." The example included with this instruction in RDA shows this clearly:

> 1:32,500,000

and if displayed in a bibliographic record this would appear as:

255   1:32,500,000

Is such data, when read in the form shown above, meaningful to users? The answer is "quite possibly yes," at least for some members of user communities, but more likely "no" for most. A best practice, and one the authors recommend following, would be to continue what has long been done according to AACR2: supply the word "Scale" in front of the RF. So, the example above would now read:

255   Scale 1:32,500,000

Determining the Scale When One Is Not Present on the Resource or Elsewhere

The concluding part of RDA 7.25.1.3 covers the four instances when a supplied phrase is used to indicate the situation with the particular map or other cartographic resource being described.

Scale Not Given

First, "if the scale cannot be determined or estimated by the means outlined in this instruction, record *Scale not given*." That is to say, if a representative fraction, verbal scale statement, or bar graph is not found on the cartographic resource or any other source of information, catalogers still need to share data with users, and to do so through well-defined, succinct statements such as this. Additionally, this part of the RDA instruction provides an alternative means to try and determine a representative fraction: comparing the resource being described with another one that is similar and using the scale from that comparative resource. The Library of Congress, in its policy statement for this part of the instruction, however, recommends *not* following this practice; the authors agree because it is a very imprecise method, and also more often than not there is not a comparative map or other resource at hand.

255   Scale not given

Note that in this example this may be the only data in the field, or the scale statement could be followed by a statement of projection or a set of coordinates or both.

Digital cartographic resources follow the same pattern used with non-digital or hardcopy resources—that is, if a scale statement is present in some form it must appear in the record in representative fraction form, but if not, then "Scale not given" can be used.

For digital resources, record the scale if:

a) the resource has a scale statement

or

b) the scale is already recorded as part of the title proper or other title information.

If scale information for a digital resource is not found in a scale statement or as part of the title proper or other title information, record "Scale not given."

Not Drawn to Scale

Next, it is important to know that not all maps are drawn or constructed with a representative distance, or scale, in mind. A classic example is the subway map, which

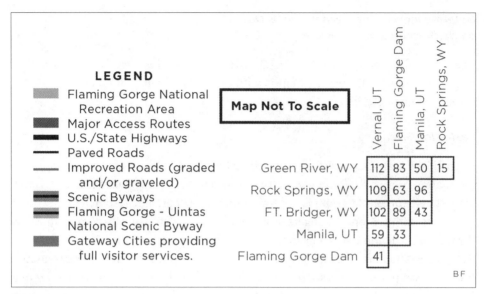

The table in the figure:

	Vernal, UT	Flaming Gorge Dam	Manila, UT	Rock Springs, WY
Green River, WY	112	83	50	15
Rock Springs, WY	109	63	96	
FT. Bridger, WY	102	89	43	
Manila, UT	59	33		
Flaming Gorge Dam	41			

Figure 4.4
"Map not to scale" example from an actual map titled "Flaming Gorge Country"

is visually a set of lines with dots or similar symbols representing subway stations shown along the way. The important thing for the user of this kind of map is to know how many "stops" it takes to get from point A to point B, including if it is necessary to get off at a given station to transfer to a different subway line to continue a journey. Distance does not need to be a factor in this kind of map. Subway maps do not explicitly share that they are not drawn to a particular scale, but other maps do, using a statement like the one shown in figure 4.4 above (actual phrasing may vary).

The appropriate part of RDA 7.25.1.3 for this situation states if the cartographic content is not drawn to scale, record "Not drawn to scale," which would be shown as:

255   Not drawn to scale

In this circumstance a projection would also never be applied. However, the cataloger can and should supply a set of coordinates; thus a $c might also appear in the field, such as shown below.

255   Not drawn to scale $c (W 110°59′--W 108°59′/N 41°37′--N 40°21′).

The coordinates above represent the area shown on the Flaming Gorge Country map.

Scale Varies and Scales Differ

RDA 7.25.1.4 covers the last two situations in which a phrase is supplied as a scale statement, depending on the circumstances (described below). It is still possible to record representative fractions in either case.

The first of these situations is a rare one, that of scale varying or changing within a single main map. These types of maps do exist, most usually created by companies in Europe that wish to show the central part of the map at a larger scale (in greater detail) than the rest of the map at the outer edges (in less detail). The intent is usually to highlight the more tourist-worthy area of a city where such things as cathedrals or other historic buildings and sites exist. There are two types of these maps. One shows a set of representative fractions as a range of scales, such as in the example shown with this instruction:

1:15,000–1:25,000

which in turn appears in the record as:

255   Scale 1:15,000–1:25,000

The second alternative is the case in which a range of scales is not provided but it is obvious from close inspection that the map was created in this manner. It is in this second situation (where RFs are not given) that the phrase "Scale varies" is used, as provided for in RDA 7.25.1.4: "If the scale within one image, map, etc., varies and the largest and smallest values are known, record both scales separated by a hyphen. If the values are not known, record *Scale varies*." A critical difference between this part of the instruction and the next part, as we indicated previously, is that it *applies to a single map*.

The last situation is the opposite of the above "Scale varies" situation in that it is very common. The critical thing to be aware of this time is that it *applies to two or more main maps*. This covers a variety of circumstances—all on a single sheet, on individual sheets, or even a mix of the two. There is a method that can be applied here as well: "If the resource consists of more than one image, map, etc., and the main images, maps, etc., are of more than one scale, record *Scales differ*" (RDA 7.25.1.4). Or "record each scale separately" according to the alternative given in 7.25.1.4.

What are the conditions that govern applying the phrase "Scales differ" versus recording each scale separately?

- If there are only two different scales, one of which may fall under the "Scale not given" circumstance, then record them both, each in its own separate 255 field.
- If there are three or more main maps, each with its own scale (including if the situation is that one or more of these falls under "Scale not given"), *either* use the supplied phrase "Scales differ" *or* record each separately following the alternative. Use the title as a guide in helping to decide; if three or four places are noted in the title then follow the order in which they are given by providing three or four scale statements in the same order, otherwise simply use the supplied phrase "Scales differ." Ultimately, it is cataloger's judgment as to how many scale statements to provide.

To be explicit, do not mix and match the use of the supplied phrase and actual scale statements in one record; the instruction is written to mean that either one *or* the other should be used.

    255   Scales differ
    or
    255   Scale 1:35,000
    255   Scale 1:28,500
    255   Scale 1:130,000

This example might represent three main maps, two of which are city maps and one a county map, all found on one or both sides of the same sheet or even on individual sheets.

To summarize, provide one or more scale statements for one or more main maps in the bibliographic record. However, the cartographic resource or resources may not show a scale, in which case supply one of four specific phrases that explain the circumstance well (although in a couple of cases there are alternatives that the cataloger may follow).

The major changes to this data element are:

- to stop using an abbreviation to represent the word "approximately"
- that we no longer supply square brackets to enclose the results of a verbal scale or to enclose both the word approximately (formerly its abbreviation) and the ratio when recording a statement derived from a bar scale

Finally, although the instructions are silent on this matter, to make it clear what this element is about, as well as what it is, the authors recommend that the statement itself begin with the word "Scale."

Dealing with Cartographic Projections

255$b CARTOGRAPHIC PROJECTION

As mentioned at the beginning of this section, inclusion of the cartographic projection data element is considered a "core if" situation. The important aspect in terms of bibliographic description is whether a projection statement appears on the resource or not. If it does appear, then record it; if it does not, move on to the next element. It is as simple as that. The data itself is placed in $b of the 255 field, following a scale statement, and if using ISBD punctuation the two subfields are separated by a space-semicolon-space (see RDA appendix D.1.2.4.1).

The scope note in RDA 7.26.1.1 provides a succinct definition of what a cartographic projection is: "Projection of cartographic content is the method or system used to represent the surface of the Earth or of a celestial sphere on a plane." The good thing for the cataloger is that it is not necessary to know why a given projection was chosen for the creation of the cartographic resource, nor what the different kinds of projections are, nor how they are applied.

The source of information for this element is given in RDA 7.26.1.2: "Take information on the projection of cartographic content from any source within the resource." Note that this information must be a part of the resource itself, its container, or an accompanying resource; if found outside of the resource (those areas noted in RDA 2.2.4) then it is not to be provided in 255$b, though could be in a note.

A cartographic projection statement is a recorded element, just as is the scale statement. According to RDA 7.26.1.3: "Record the projection of cartographic content if considered important for identification or selection." Any other details of cartographic content, such as a statement about an ellipsoid or orientation of north, would appear in a note, according to RDA 7.27.1.3. It is good practice to always record the type of projection if present on the resource.

Examples of Common Projection Statements

> Universal Transverse Mercator projection
> Polyconic projection
> Albers equal-area projection

As a reminder, do not abbreviate the word "projection" when recording such a statement, because it is not one of the terms found in table B.7 in appendix B.

RDA 7.26.1.3 also includes an optional addition about statements of parallels and meridians that sometimes accompany a statement of projection on a cartographic resource: "Record phrases about meridians and/or parallels that are associated with the projection statement. Record information about ellipsoids as other details of cartographic content (see 7.27)." LC practice is to record data about parallels and meridians (see the LC-PCC PS for 7.26.1.3).

Examples of projection statements with meridian or parallels information would include:

> Transverse Mercator projection, central meridian 35°13′30″E
> Azimuthal equidistant projection centered on Nicosia, N 35°10′, E 33°22′

To reiterate, if a projection statement is found on the cartographic resource, its container, or an accompanying resource, it should be recorded in the 255$b. If no statement can be found, ignore this element and move on to providing coordinates (in which case there would be no $b in the 255 field).

Coordinates for Cartographic Resources and Their Applications

What are "coordinates" and why are they important to the bibliographic description? This is not a core element in RDA unless the cataloger's institution is the Library of Congress or a PCC program member, or is following the LC-PCC PS, but the authors recommend attempting to always supply either bounding box or point (*x,y*) coordinates. Accordingly, this discussion is divided into two sections, one covering the traditional method of deriving coordinate values from the resource itself and one discussing methods of finding and using coordinates from alternative sources outside of the resource itself. The latter methodology lends itself well to discovering a set of coordinates for a given location and painlessly inserting the data into the bibliographic record.

To answer the "what is" part of the question, turn to the scope statement in RDA 7.4.1.1, which states that "coordinates of cartographic content is a mathematical system for identifying the area covered by the cartographic content of a resource." In addition, this scope statement states that coordinates are expressed as latitude and longitude on the Earth's or a planet's surface, or by means of angles of right ascension and declination for celestial cartographic content. Indeed, the common conversational phrase associated with coordinates is expressed by "lat/long" or "latitude and longitude," so if someone is talking about latitude and longitude it has to do with an area or point on the Earth's surface with numerical coordinate values representing that area or point.

DERIVING COORDINATES FROM THE RESOURCE ITSELF

RDA 7.4.1.2 covers sources of information for coordinates data: "Take information on the coordinates of cartographic content from any source within the resource. If information on the coordinates of cartographic content is not provided within the resource, take the information from any source."

Besides understanding latitude and longitude and being able to derive coordinates in the form of degrees, minutes, and seconds, the next very important step is mastering the proper method for *recording* sets of these data points. RDA 7.4.1.3 explains how to do this:

> For terrestrial cartographic content, record the coordinates either
>
> a) by recording longitude and latitude (see RDA 7.4.2)
>
> *or*
>
> b) by recording strings of coordinate pairs (see RDA 7.4.3).
>
> For celestial cartographic content, record the right ascension and declination (see RDA 7.4.4).

Most catalogers will be working with terrestrial (surface of the Earth or other celestial body) coordinates primarily or exclusively. This means following one of the two methods noted in a) or b) above, and traditionally the first choice is used. This takes us to the instruction on recording longitude and latitude in RDA 7.4.2 and its sub-instructions.

Once the bounding box coordinates on the map have been found, or corner coordinates are determined by an extrapolation method in order to make sure the entire geographic area in question is surrounded without losing data, it is time to record the data (i.e., the geographic area in question) in a very specific manner. RDA 7.4.2.3 nicely covers this methodology:

1. Record coordinates in the order of westernmost, easternmost, northernmost, and southernmost in the 255$c. An easier way to remember the order of these elements is always to record from left to right first—these are longitude coordinates going either West or East from the prime meridian passing through Greenwich, England, which serves as the starting point for either direction and is the zero-degree (0°) line of longitude—and then from top to bottom next (these are latitude coordinates going either North or South from the Equator, which is the zero-degree (0°) line of latitude). "Record the coordinates for longitude and latitude as sexagesimal coordinates, using degrees (°), minutes ('), and seconds ("). For longitude, use the Greenwich prime meridian as the reference meridian." If using the ALA Character Set, these symbols can be located by name: "degree symbol" for degrees, the "Miagkii znak" for minutes, and the "Tverdyi znak" for seconds.

2. Within the string of coordinates in 255$c there will be one pair of longitude coordinates, which may be West (W) and West (W), West (W) and East (E), or East (E) and East (E) depending on the location of the geographic area of the resource on the globe. That will be followed by a pair of latitude coordinates, which may be North (N) and North (N), North (N) and South (S), or South (S) and South (S), again depending on the location of the geographic area and its location on the globe: "Precede each coordinate by W, E, N, or S, as appropriate" and also "separate the west and east coordinates with a hyphen and the north and south coordinates with a hyphen."

3. When recording the coordinates statement using ISBD, the entire statement is enclosed in a set of parentheses, as noted in RDA D.1.2.4.1: "Enclose the statement of coordinates and equinox in one pair of parentheses."

In the following examples, those recorded without parentheses follow RDA 7.4.2.3, followed by an example of how they would appear in the 255 field with ISBD punctuation included:

Statement of Coordinates Alone	Statement of Coordinates as Part of a Mathematical Data Statement	
E 79°--E 86°/N 20°--N 12°	255	Scale 1:100,000 ; $b polyconic projection $c (E 79°--E 86°/N 20°--N 12°).
E 15°00′00″--E 17°30′45″/N 1°30′12″--S 2°30′35″	255	Scale approximately 1:20,000 $c (E 15°00′00″--E 17°30′45″/N 1°30′12″--S 2°30′35″).
W 74°50′--W 74°40′/N 45°05′--N 45°00′	255	Scale 1:600 $c (W 74°50′--W 74°40′/N 45°05′--N 45°00′).

In the examples above, the first map (or cartographic image) would be located in southern India, the second would be a small area of central Africa, and the third would be a locale right on the border between northern New York State and southern Québec, Canada. Note that in the first example on the globe India is east of Greenwich (Eastern Hemisphere) and north of the Equator (Northern Hemisphere); in the second central Africa is east of Greenwich but straddling the Equator; and finally in the last example New York/Québec is west of Greenwich (Western Hemisphere) and north of the Equator. For places located in Australia or New Zealand, for example, the coordinate statement would represent values that are east of Greenwich and south of the Equator, and would have directional notations of E–E for longitude and S–S for latitude.

Additional key aspects of recording coordinates that are not in the instructions include:

- Be consistent in recording the set of numerical values as shown above. In the first example all values are in degrees only; in the second example all show degrees, minutes, and seconds combined; and in the third example all show only degrees and minutes combined. Do *not* "mix and match" numerical values across the statement as shown in the example below:

  255   Scale 1:50,000 $c (W 82°30′--W 76°/N 33°20′05″--N 30°10′).

  Rather, to illustrate the correct way that this set of coordinates is to be recorded, using zeroes as placeholders, this statement would appear as:

  255   Scale 1:50,000 $c (W 82°30′00″--W 76°00′00″/N 33°20′05″--N 30°10′00″).

- Record point coordinates in the 255 field (*x,y*) for large-scale places such as for city maps by placing the point of longitude coordinate (*x*) to the left of the forward slash and the point of latitude coordinate (*y*) to the right of the forward slash as shown in the example below. However, when recording the four 034 subfields for this data (subfields d, e, f, and g) simply repeat each of the coordinate points across the string as shown below.

Point coordinates for the city of Williamsport, Pennsylvania:

034 1   a $b 9400 $d W0770004 $e W0770004 $f N0411428 $g N0411428
255   Scale approximately 1:9,400 $c (W 77°00′04″/N 41°14′28″).

To find comprehensive details regarding how to record scale, projection, and coordinate data elements in both the 255 and 034 fields, see appendix D.

The preceding discussions demonstrate the means of recording coordinates using what is known as the sexagesimal system of degrees, minutes, and seconds based on the Earth being measured as 360° in circumference. However, RDA 7.4.2.3 concludes with instructions for recording coordinates using the decimal system, which is more commonly used within software applications such as geographic information systems (GIS) and is provided in this form for easier machine manipulation. Going forward it is possible that the preferred method for recording coordinates will become the decimal system method. For now, most catalogers will continue to follow the instructions using the sexagesimal system. An example from RDA of a coordinates statement using the decimal system is:

W 95.15°--W 74.35°/N 56.85°--N 41.73°

In applying this to the bibliographic record, once again according to ISBD punctuation, the entire statement would be enclosed in parentheses. Note that the LC-PCC PS included in this part of the RDA instruction for preferring one or the other of the two systems is to follow whichever is used in the resource itself. Generally speaking, hardcopy cartographic resources show coordinates in the familiar degrees, minutes, and seconds format, while digital resources display them in decimal form.

DERIVING COORDINATES FROM NON-PREFERRED OR ALTERNATE SOURCES

It is worth repeating a recommendation noted at the beginning of this section on coordinates: every cataloger creating a bibliographic description for a cartographic resource should endeavor to include a coordinates statement whenever possible. Under RDA 7.4.2 this is not a core element except for catalogers at the Library of Congress or for those catalogers who catalog according to the BIBCO standard in the Program for Cooperative Cataloging (see the LC-PCC PS for this instruction). However, at this point in time and moving forward, coordinates play a key role in digital cartographic resources, both within the resources themselves and more broadly within the geographic community and across other disciplines. The ability to merge cartographic resources with other kinds of resources in the online environment requires a key set of data: coordinate values. It has become very easy for catalogers to supply these values, thus empowering others to create new knowledge in meaningful ways with location as a basis of understanding.

Understandably, this can often be a tedious process when using the methodology of taking coordinates from the resource itself, unless the coordinates for the four corners of the map are provided. Extrapolating one or more coordinate values when a line of longitude or latitude slices through a portion of the geographic area being described is time-consuming and an "unfriendly," though not difficult, process to learn. To speed that process of garnering bounding box coordinates when they do not appear at the corners, it is often possible to turn to a world atlas, look up the continent, country, state, etc., involved, and simply borrow the resultant coordinates from that resource (though often still extrapolating to a certain degree). When creating a full-level bibliographic record under AACR2 the rule was that if the coordinates appeared as a part of the resource, including them in the description was required. If no coordinates appeared on the resource, catalogers could choose to leave coordinates out of the record entirely, or use a method similar to the one described above employing an atlas to discover and put them in the record. Now this process is very much simpler.

SEEKING POINT OR X, Y COORDINATE VALUES ONLINE

For cartographic resources that show a relatively or actually small geographic area—a "large scale map"—two online resources can be employed to garner point coordinates.

The first is GEOnet, the United States Board on Geographic Names' database for foreign places, which is hosted by the National Geospatial-Intelligence Agency. This database is used for all places around the world except for Antarctica and the United States. For place names in Antarctica and the United States, catalogers refer to the Geographic Names Information System (GNIS), which is hosted by the United States Geological Survey. In both of these databases it is possible to search for an administrative place (populated place or civil area) or a geographic feature (river, mountain, lake, etc.). Search results will display point coordinates for a city, town, village, mountain, river, etc., as x, y or point coordinates; for administrative places these coordinates are considered the geographic "center" of said city, town, or village. These can then be placed into the bibliographic record as described previously. For example, searching for the city of Bremerton, Washington state, shows the point coordinates for this place as:

> 473402N [and] 1223758W

> (coordinates are displayed within a table separated by a line)

which would be recorded when describing a map of this place as:

> 034 1   a $b 25000 $d W1223758 $e W1223758 $f N0473402 $g N0473402
> 255   Scale 1:25,000 $c (W 122°37′58″/N 47°34′02″).

SEEKING BOUNDING BOX COORDINATES ONLINE

A recently developed and powerful online tool known as the Klokan Bounding Box Tool virtually eliminates any excuse for not including coordinates that are not found on the resource itself.

This easy-to-use tool combines a fill-in-the-box search feature and a world map in which it is possible to pull and drag the resulting bounding box edges around, if needed, to accommodate non-administrative areas shown on a map such as those for a portion of a state or province, or a mountain range or similar region. Or, if simply seeking the bounding-box coordinates for an administrative area, the results will show as a box with a grayed-in area on the map representing the place needed. Accompanying this visual result is a set of bounding-box coordinates shown in its own results box below the map image. To the left of this results box is a pull-down menu that can be set so that the coordinates themselves display in a standard form such as OCLC (called the "MARC-OCLC" format in the list). From here it is possible to copy and paste the coordinates string (including subfield tags), into the 034 field, then come back and copy and paste the coordinates statement (including parentheses and subfield tag) that belongs in the 255 field. With this new online tool every cataloger will be able to derive a set of bounding-box coordinates for at least 90 percent of all cartographic resources being described very easily.

264 FIELD: PRODUCTION, PUBLICATION, DISTRIBUTION, MANUFACTURE, AND COPYRIGHT NOTICE

This field encompasses the following RDA instructions:

2.7 Production Statement

2.8 Publication Statement

2.9 Distribution Statement

2.10 Manufacture Statement

2.11 Copyright Date Statement

One can determine which of these data elements or portions of them are core by turning to RDA 1.3. In particular, the different types of dates fall into "core if" categories. These will be examined in more depth below.

Production, publication, distribution, and manufacturer's statements are all to be transcribed from the resource according to RDA 2.7.1.4, 2.8.1.4, 2.9.1.4, and 2.10.1.4. In AACR2, we were accustomed to heavily abbreviating words in these areas, particularly those such as "Dept." or "Co."; now these must be transcribed from the resource. Copyright symbols or words should also be transcribed.

Unlike in AACR2, where the different kinds of imprint-type elements fall into one field (MARC 260) and are segregated based on subfields, RDA has provided one repeatable field to accommodate the five different kinds of data elements noted in the preceding paragraph. Thus, it is possible for two or three 264 fields to be employed in the bibliographic record to cover a specific circumstance. For contemporary cartographic resources, the most common data type found on the resource is publication information, and the second is a copyright statement. All five of the different 264 field types are available for use in cataloging cartographic items, and can be mixed and matched to fit the need.

Methodology and Structure of the 264 Field

The best way to get comfortable with this brand-new MARC field is to learn its component parts and become familiar with how it operates. And the best place to get a clear understanding of this, as well as clear definitions of production, publication, distribution, manufacture, and copyright is to turn to the MARC 21 Standard for Bibliographic Data and look up the 264 field. Another key document from the Library of Congress Program for Cooperative Cataloging available online is titled "PCC Guidelines for the 264 Field" (www.loc.gov/aba/pcc/documents/264-Guidelines.doc) and is highly recommended as a resource to learn the details for this new field. Note that a "production" is defined in the MARC 21 standard for the 264 field as "a statement relating to the inscription, fabrication, construction, etc., of a resource in an unpublished form," with *unpublished form* being the paramount detail. The glossary in RDA similarly defines a "production statement" as a "statement identifying … a resource in an unpublished form." The production type of 264 field is used frequently when cataloging early cartographic items, particularly manuscript maps.

The three key aspects to applying data to these fields correctly are:

1. determining which type of information is a part of the resource, whether one or more; then
2. applying the correct Indicator value for each field; and
3. following the "pecking order" of these fields, which is what makes them "core if" elements.

The one type of 264 field that is uniquely different is copyright date, in which the date may or may not be the same as the publication, distribution, or manufacture date but is the *only* data element that goes into a 264 field coded with a "4" in the second Indicator position. Conversely, the other 264 field types include subfields in which to input place, name, and date elements. (Note that in the MARC standard there are three other subfields available for use; none of these would commonly appear with cartographic resources and thus will not be covered in detail here.)

In contrast, the first Indicator value is called the "Sequence of statements" value, and can either be coded as follows:

First Indicator value	Sequence of statements
<blank>	Earliest/Not applicable/No information provided
2	Intervening (publication information changed)
3	Current/latest

Most often these scenarios occur with serially issued resources or continuing resources, which are not that common with cartographic resources, so the vast majority of the time this first Indicator will be left blank.

Once one determines if the information is publication data, distribution data, or one of the other types (what the MARC 21 standard calls the "function of entity" type), then one can select the appropriate second Indicator value as shown in the following list:

0 = Production statement
1 = Publication statement
2 = Distribution statement
3 = Manufacture statement
4 = Copyright notice date

The data itself is entered into the appropriate subfields of the 264 field, for instance *place* of publication or manufacture appears in $a, *name* of publisher or manufacturer in $b, and so forth.

Most typically for contemporary cartographic resources, if two date types need to be represented they are usually for publication information and copyright. In the United States, federal government agencies are the largest producers of cartographic resources, and these are not copyrightable (Mazzone 2006). In contrast, there are many companies who do copyright their cartographic output, so it would not be unusual to find a publication statement that includes a publication date and a copyright statement with its copyright date. Such a resource would appear in the following manner:

264 1 Lubbock, TX : $b Word Publications, $c [2012]
264 4 $c ©2012

Also note that in the example shown above, although the 2012 date is duplicated in the description, the same date would appear in both the Date1 and Date2 fixed fields and subsequently the Type of Date (DtSt) fixed field would be coded "t" to reflect the use of both a publication date and a copyright date in the description.

Reprints of published maps are another situation encountered on occasion. For instance, the *Geologic map of Wisconsin* published in 1949 and reprinted in 1959 would receive two 264 fields, one to cover the publication statement and the other to share manufacture data:

> 264   1 [Madison, Wis.] : $b Wisconsin Geological and Natural History Survey, University of Wisconsin, $c [1949]
>
> 264   3 [Baltimore, Md.] : $b Lith. A. Hoen & Co., $c 1959.

A 1949 revision date appears in the edition field, and a quoted note indicates that the map was "Reprinted 1959."

However, a non-published cartographic resource, such as a manuscript map, would only require a single 264 field with the second Indicator set at "0" (zero).

RDA also has established a "pecking order." This imposed order, as found in the instruction for core elements (RDA 1.3), explains what to do when formal publication data are missing but data from a distribution or manufacturer statement are present. It becomes an "if-then" situation, and to use the distribution data as an example, the instruction specifies:

> Place of distribution (for a published resource, if place of publication not identified; if more than one, only the first recorded is required)
>
> Distributor's name (for a published resource, if publisher not identified; if more than one, only the first recorded is required)
>
> Date of distribution (for a published resource, if date of publication not identified)

Similar instructions are given for the manufacturer statement. Essentially, once one discovers there is no publication element data to be used, then use those for place of distribution; but if there is not publication element or distribution element data, then use the manufacture element data if present. What to do when there is no data for any of these elements is discussed in detail below.

RDA INSTRUCTIONS RELATING TO PUBLICATION-TYPE DATA

Because the process for providing the data elements for each of the different types of production, publication, distribution, and manufacture statements is similar, a single example should suffice. It will be the publication statement, which is the most common type encountered when working with cartographic resources. Instructions for handling the production, distribution, and manufacturer statements follow a similar course.

Sources of information for publication statements are provided at the specific element level (see individual instructions linked from under RDA 2.8.1.2):

1. The first instance of Place of Publication is core; other elements are optional.
2. Places of publication and publisher's names are *transcribed* from the resource, see RDA 2.8.1.4.

3. RDA 2.8.1.5 addresses *recording changes in publication statements*, which for cartographic resources likely would apply only to multipart monographic items. As per this instruction, in this circumstance one should add a note to the record indicating the scope of changes involved.

4. Place of publication is covered in RDA 2.8.2. The source of information covers three possibilities. A very important aspect of place of publication is how to record place names properly.

RECORDING PLACE NAMES APPROPRIATELY

RDA 2.8.2.3 instructs recording "the place of publication by applying the basic instructions at 2.8.1"—in other words, transcribe the place of publication as found on the resource. Include both the local place name (city, town, etc.) and the name of the larger jurisdiction or jurisdictions (state, province, etc., and/or country) if present on the source of information.

An optional addition under RDA 2.8.2.3 also permits adding any preposition appearing with the place name that is required to make sense of the statement. The example for this is "V Praze"; a similar example for an English place name would be one in which "The" appears before the name. Both of these would appear in 264$a. Another optional addition is to include a full address. However, perhaps the most important optional addition, and the one used most regularly, allows adding the name of a larger jurisdiction by supplying it in square brackets. This further identifies a local place name that could be confused with an identical place name in another location if the larger jurisdiction is not present on the resource, for example:

> Cairo [Egypt]
>
> *versus*
>
> Cairo [Ga.]

This example shows the state name in abbreviated form, which is allowed because it appears in table B.1 at RDA B.11. However, as noted in chapter 3 of this book, the authors learned that the British Library submitted a proposal to the JSC (Proposal 6JSC/BL/10/BL follow up) to remove the exception status for place names in resource descriptions and name headings. If this proposal is accepted and implemented, then the supplied place name would appear as:

> Cairo [Georgia]

What happens when a resource has more than one place of publication? RDA 2.8.2.4 instructs the cataloger to "record the place names in the order indicated by the sequence, layout, or typography of the names on the source of information" and then provides more detail in an "if-then" statement. Basically, this boils down to "take what you see." However, this instruction also tells us what to do with multiple publishers and their accompanying places of publication: "If there are two or more publishers, and there are two or more places associated with one or more of the publishers then record the place names associated with each publisher in the order indicated by the sequence, layout, or typography of the place names on the source of information."

DEALING WITH MISSING DATA

The opposite problem—a lack of data such as place of publication—occurs frequently when describing cartographic resources. RDA 2.8.2.6 addresses this conundrum. The cataloger then begins the process of supplying information, which necessarily entails using square brackets and potentially dealing with the abbreviated place names that are allowed by RDA appendix B:

> If the place of publication is not identified in the resource, supply the place of publication or probable place of publication. Apply the instructions in this order of preference:
>
> a) known place (see RDA 2.8.2.6.1)
>
> b) probable place (see RDA 2.8.2.6.2)
>
> c) known country, state, province, etc. (see RDA 2.8.2.6.3)
>
> d) probable country, state, province, etc. (see RDA 2.8.2.6.4).
>
> Indicate that the information was taken from a source outside the resource itself (see RDA 2.2.4).

In other words, use square brackets and, if needed for explanation, include a note describing the situation.

Well-known place names are frequently supplied with cartographic resources, particularly those that have been published. These can be garnered fairly easily from clues on or with the map or other resources, or through online research. A cataloger may "supply the local place name (city, town, etc.)" and also "include the name of the larger jurisdiction if necessary for identification." It is wise to include the name of a larger jurisdiction for cartographic resources; because so many place names occur in different locations around the world, this addition narrows the local place name provided down to a specific location. Examples might be:

> [Salem, Mass.]
> [Cairo, Egypt]
> [Paris, France]

RDA 2.8.2.6.2 addresses another possibility for identifying a place when the cataloger may not be able to identify a specific place of publication but feels there is enough evidence to name a *probable* place. Because the data is supplied it must go in square brackets, but this time it is also necessary to add a question mark to indicate lack of certainty.

[Port Alberni, B.C.?]

A similar situation also occurs with cartographic resources—providing a probable country, state, province, etc., when lacking a local place, based on evidence or even a cataloger's experience with the map-publishing world. There may be little information found in the resource itself or other sources of information, but the cataloger feels certain that the map was at least published within a given larger jurisdiction (e.g., a country). According to RDA 2.8.2.6.3, "if the probable local place is unknown, supply the name of the country, state, province, etc., of publication."

[Norway]

The last of these four situations is similar to when a probable country, state, province, etc., similar to the above, is known, only at a level of less certainty. Again, supply the data but use a question mark to indicate uncertainty:

[Denmark?]

If all of the steps just walked through fail to turn up any idea of a place of publication, RDA has come up with a manner in which to tell the user of the record that the data simply is not available. Supply the phrase "Place of publication not identified" in square brackets:

264 1   [Place of publication not identified] (see RDA 2.8.2.6)

In a sense, this is not so different from using AACR2 rule 1.4C6: "If no place or probable place can be given, give *S.l.* (sine loco), or its equivalent in a nonroman script," except this method supplies a phrase that is understood by everyone who reads English, as opposed to an abbreviation of a Latin term understood only by librarians and scholars. Still, try to identify a place of publication according to one of the sources of information, or one of the preceding techniques, before using this last method. In other words, use this technique as a last resort.

Note that the supplied phrases for the lack of name and/or date information are very similar to the one given above for place:

[publisher not identified] (see RDA 2.8.4.7)
[date of publication not identified] (see RDA 2.8.6.6)

And once again, in the case of a missing name of publisher, an AACR2 Latin abbreviation, *s.n.* (sine nomine), was changed to a clearer English phrase that users will better understand.

However, there is an LC-PCC PS for RDA 2.8.6.6 associated with the situation when a date is lacking from the resource. This is an important policy statement because it illustrates how to supply an inferred date under multiple scenarios (using square brackets, of course). First the policy statement tells the cataloger to prefer the use of an inferred date over the use of the supplied phrase noted above, "Supply a date of publication if possible, using the guidelines below, rather than give '[date of publication not identified]'. Follow the instructions in 1.9.2 for supplied dates, including the use of the question mark with probable dates." It would be wise to learn how to handle unknown dates of publication in this manner because it happens frequently with cartographic resources. RDA 1.9.2 includes a list of methods for inferring a date of publication, whether that is from a known copyright date to other kinds of dates found, such as one for distribution or manufacture.

The pattern followed in determining place of publication data for the 264 field involves going from transcribing data found on the cartographic resource to a last resort of supplying a standard phrase in a set of square brackets. The process for inputting the name and date of publisher, distributor, or manufacturer follows the same pattern; just follow the RDA instructions under the numbers provided at the beginning of this section. And remember that place, name, and date for all of these categories is core in RDA (see RDA 1.3 for specifics).

COPYRIGHT DATE

As stated previously, copyright dates are treated differently in RDA. When present, they always appear in their own 264 field with the second Indicator value set to "4":

> 264　4 $c ©1998

Unlike the other four statements, the only data appearing in a 264 for a copyright date circumstance is the copyright date itself—do not input place and/or name data here. An example of record content that includes both a publication statement and a copyright date statement used in tandem is shown in the very first example of this section above. The PCC Guidelines for the 264 field also helpfully lists the treatment of $c data, or "date" data, as follows:

Subfield $c (Date of Production, Publication, Distribution, Manufacture, or Copyright Notice):

Subfield $c may appear in more than one 264 field when:

- A copyright notice date is being given in addition to date of production, publication, distribution, manufacture.
- Multiple statements for different functions are being recorded, in which case $c may be recorded once for each function. For example, $c may appear in one and only one 264 with second indicator 0, one and only one 264 with second indicator 1, etc.

Otherwise, for serials and multipart monographs, subfield "c" should appear in the 264 field with the first indicator left blank (Not applicable/No information provided/

Earliest) and/or second indicator 4 (Copyright Notice Date). It may be absent if the description is not based on first/earliest issue or part.

300 FIELD: PHYSICAL DESCRIPTION

Note that this section will cover four of the subfields in the MARC bibliographic format for this field. The remaining subfields are not commonly used for cartographic resources. The illustrations in this section come from *Cartographic Materials: A Manual of Interpretation for AACR2, Second Edition, Revised.*

Background to Physical Description

- Extent is a core element (RDA 3.4.2) if the resource is complete.
- Other physical details are "core if" and LC-PCC core.
- Dimensions is a core element (other than for serials and online electronic resources, core for LC).

The four data elements that appear in the MARC 300 field are the extent of the item in $a, other physical details in $b, dimensions in $c, and accompanying material in $e. The text below will follow this order as well, because this is how many catalogers approach completing this field.

How to record extent is discussed primarily in the RDA 3.4.1 Basic Instructions on Recording Extent. Cartographic resources are covered specifically in RDA 3.4.2.

Instructions concerning other physical details are in a multitude of sections in RDA chapters 3 and 7. The sections of most interest to cartographic resource catalogers are:

3.6 Base materials
3.8 Mount
3.9 Production method
3.11 Layout
3.14 Polarity
7.17 Colour Content

Instructions for dimensions are at RDA 3.5.2. Additionally, instructions to describe accompanying materials can be found in RDA 3.1.4, most notably and clearly in the LC-PCC PS for 3.1.4, and if needed to describe the relationship between the resource and its accompanying material, appendix J 2.5. Methods to determine the extent of the map, record the physical details, and measure the dimensions of the map are almost the same in RDA as in AACR2. A major change is that extent is considered a core element in RDA only if the resource is complete or if the total extent is known. However, current best practice is to continue to record a 300 field for cartographic resources because most fall within one of these two circumstances.

300$a EXTENT OF CARTOGRAPHIC RESOURCE

How to record extent is covered in RDA 3.4.2.2, which states: "Record the extent of the resource by giving the number of units and an appropriate term from the following list. Record the term in the singular or plural, as applicable: atlas, diagram, globe, map, model, profile, remote-sensing image, section or view." If there is more than one type of unit, record the number of each applicable type. If the number of units is not easy to ascertain, then record an estimated number preceded by the term *approximately*.

> EXAMPLE
>
> 300   2 maps

> EXAMPLE
>
> 300   Approximately 200 maps

Because cartographic resources appear in many different forms, it is permissible to use a concise term or terms from another source list to indicate the specific unit type if the list given in RDA 3.4.2.2 does not adequately convey the unit being described. In such cases, refer to the lists for extent of still images at RDA 3.4.4.2 or for three-dimensional forms at 3.4.6.2 if they are applicable.

> EXAMPLE
>
> 300   1 jigsaw puzzle

It is also fairly common for there to be one map on multiple sheets or multiple maps on one sheet. RDA 3.4.2.3 mandates recording the number of cartographic units and to specify the number of sheets in these cases.

> EXAMPLE
>
> 300   5 maps on 1 sheet

> EXAMPLE
>
> 300   1 map on 2 sheets

Similarly, if a cartographic unit is presented in more than one segment and meant to be fitted together to form one or more cartographic units and all the segments are on one sheet, then record the number of complete cartographic units followed by "in," and then give the number of segments (RDA 3.4.2.4). The most common example of this is the Instituto Geográfico Militar's *Mapa de Chile* that divides the country into three segments (see figure 4.5).

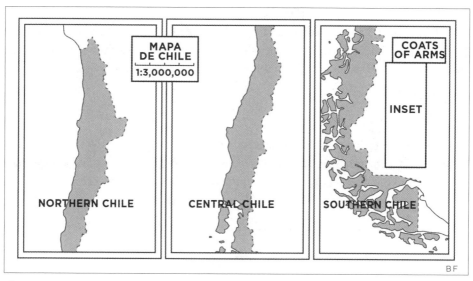

Figure 4.5
Instituto Geográfico Militar's Mapa de Chile showing one map
printed in segments on one sheet

Its extent is as follows:

EXAMPLE

300   1 map in 3 segments

Atlases are, of course, treated differently, as explained in RDA 3.4.2.5. The number of pages or volumes is to be included in parentheses after the term "atlas," as given in the list at RDA 3.4.2.2.

EXAMPLE

1 atlas (2 volumes)

Note that in accordance with the instructions covered in chapter 3 of this manual, "volumes" is no longer abbreviated.

300$b OTHER PHYSICAL DETAILS

Color

The most common "other physical detail" recorded in bibliographic records for cartographic resources is that the resource was created using two or more colors. The instructions for recording color content are found at RDA 7.17.1, which defines "colour content" as the presence of color, tone, etc., in the content of the resource. The determination of whether or not a resource is colored is based on the evidence presented by the resource itself. However, there are limits to what evidence is admissible. RDA 7.17.1.3 specifies disregarding colored material outside the actual content of the resource, and gives the example of the border of a map. So if the map is in black and white and the border is red, the map is considered uncolored.

EXAMPLE

300   1 map : $b color

However, the term "colored" is used only when the map has had its color applied by hand. Maps that are hand-colored are often manuscript in nature or antiquarian resources and this fact is also recorded in the other physical details area.

EXAMPLE

300   1 map : $b manuscript, colored

Base Materials

Although most modern maps are printed on paper, maps have been created using a variety of materials. When the material the map is printed or drawn on is *not* paper, RDA 3.6.1.3 instructs the cataloger to "record the base material if considered important for identification or selection." There is a lengthy list of terms to be used along with a directive that if none of the terms given is appropriate, employ another concise term or terms to indicate the material used.

EXAMPLE

300   1 map : $b color, silk

Mount

RDA 3.8.1.1 defines "mount" as "the physical material used for the support or backing to which the base material of a resource has been attached." Again, record the material used for the backing if considered important for identification or selection. Refer to the list of terms at RDA 3.6.1.3 for appropriate terminology. Further details about the mounting can be recorded in a note, if desired. Also, if there is evidence that the map was mounted on a backing locally, then the information about the material used should be recorded in a local note only.

EXAMPLE

300   1 map : $b color, linen

Layout

Although it is often the case that a map is printed on one side of one sheet, there are occasions where one map is printed on both sides of one sheet or there are two maps printed on each side of one sheet. RDA 3.11.1.3 instructs the cataloger to record the layout of the resource. And, once again, there is a list of terms, this time broken down by type of resource. The two terms given for cartographic image are "both sides" and "back to back." "Both sides" is used when there is one map that starts on one side of the sheet and continues at the same scale on the other side, or when there are two different main maps with each map printed on its own side of the sheet. "Back to back" is used when the *same map* is printed on each side of a single sheet in a different language.

EXAMPLE

300   1 map : $b both sides, color

EXAMPLE

300   2 maps on 1 sheet : $b both sides, color

EXAMPLE

300   2 maps on 1 sheet : $b back to back, color

Production Method

There are certain categories of maps that libraries commonly receive that are not commercially printed. For instance, many state agencies issue maps that are photocopies, blueline prints, blueprints, or blackline prints. RDA 3.9.1.3 instructs the cataloger to record the production method if considered important. Again, there is a list of preferred terms but if none of the terms is appropriate, a concise term or terms can be used.

EXAMPLE

300   1 map : $b blueline

Polarity

Polarity is defined in RDA 3.14.1.1 as the relationship of the colors and tones in an image to the colors and tones of the object reproduced. This commonly comes into play for cartographic resources created as reproductions such as blueline and blackline prints, blueprints, and remote-sensing images.

EXAMPLE

300   1 map : $b blackline, negative

300$c DIMENSIONS

Providing the dimensions of a map is not always a straightforward enterprise. An entire section of RDA is dedicated to the process of recording dimensions. RDA 3.5 refers us to the basic instructions for recording dimensions, while 3.5.2 and its sub-instructions are specific to recording dimensions under different circumstances. Fortunately, the actual manner used to measure the map and/or its container is not different from the method used in AACR2. Therefore, this section will draw heavily on the dimensions areas from *Cartographic Materials* (2002 revision, pages 5–32 through 5–45) while bringing past practice in line with RDA.

Of note in the examples below is the lack of a period at the end of "cm" when it falls as the last data element in the string. While some catalogers may feel that period should be in place as a means of indicating a "stop" to the string of text, there is an instance when a period *should* appear here. Item number 4 of the LC-PCC PS for RDA 1.7.1 says that field 300 "may end in no punctuation, may end in a right parenthesis when the last element of the field is a parenthetical qualifier, or may end in a period when the last element is an abbreviation. When a record has a 490 field, insure that field 300 ends in a period." Once again, to be consistent in displaying the symbol for centimeters, do *not* include a period at the end of the MARC 300 field when it ends in this symbol, but be aware of and follow the exception.

The face of the map is still measured from within the neat lines, first recording height and secondly width (see figure 4.6). If the map is round, measure its diameter

EXAMPLE

300   1 map : $b color ; $c 60 x 66 cm

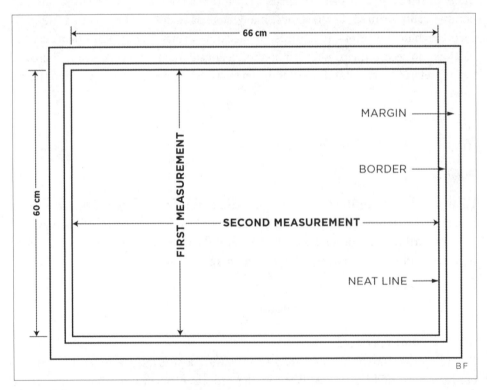

Figure 4.6
Map measurements example showing "neat line," "border," and "margins"

and indicate in the 300$c that it is the diameter (see figure 4.7). Continue the practice of rounding up to the nearest centimeter for modern maps and to the nearest tenth of a centimeter for early printed and manuscript sheet maps (see RDA 3.5.2.2).

EXAMPLE

300   1 map : $b color ; $c 50 cm in diameter

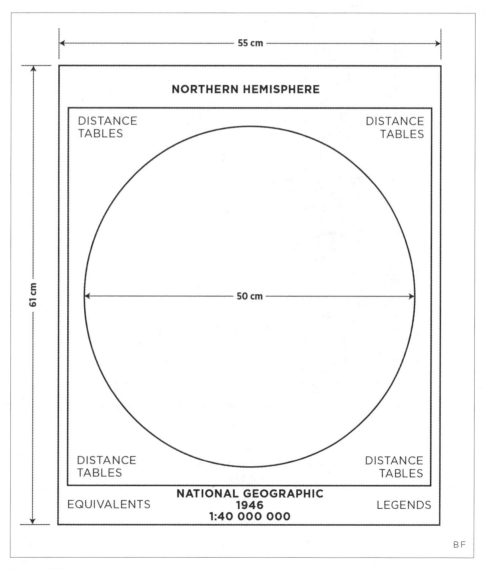

Figure 4.7
Map measurements example of a circular map

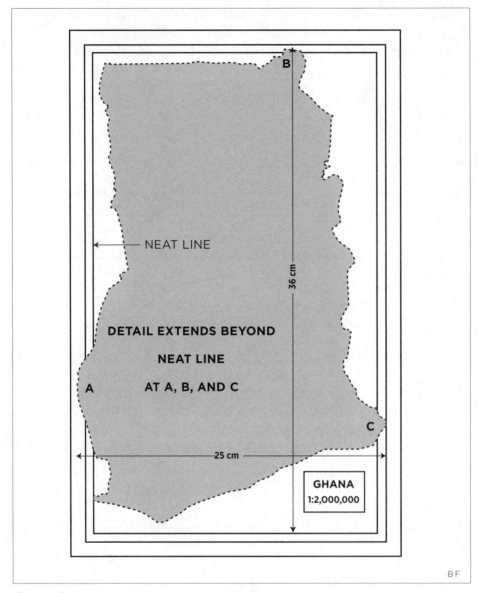

Figure 4.8
Map measurements example showing a "bleeding edge" or when some
cartographic detail extends beyond the neat line

If the cartographic detail of the map extends beyond the neat lines, include those details in the dimensions of the map (see figure 4.8).

EXAMPLE

300   1 map : $b color ; $c 36 x 25 cm

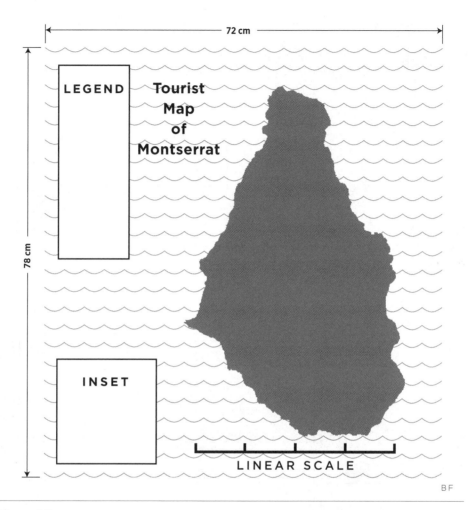

Figure 4.9
Map measurements example showing a "bleeding edge" all around

There are times when the map does not have a neat line, it has an irregular shape, or the map bleeds to the edge of the sheet. In such cases record just the dimensions of the sheet, as shown above in figure 4.9 and recorded as in the example below. However, it is permissible to choose to measure the greatest dimensions of the geographic area instead. If providing the size of geographic area, then also record the dimensions of the sheet following those dimensions.

    300   1 map : $b color ; $c on sheet 78 x 72 cm

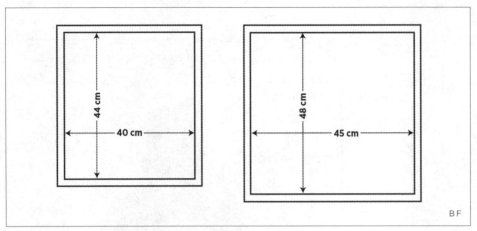

Figure 4.10
Map measurements example when dealing with two sizes
of maps in a series or collection

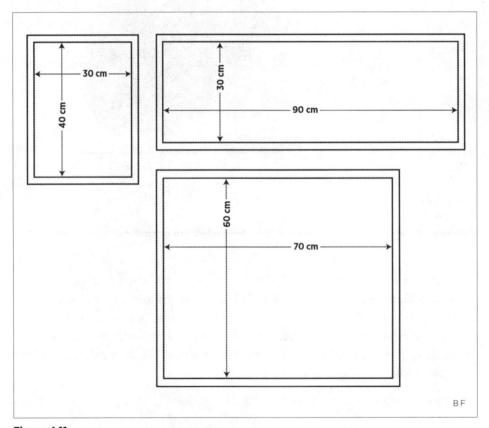

Figure 4.11
Map measurements example when dealing with more than two sizes
of maps in a series or collection

Maps can also be printed on multiple sheets. These sheets can be the same, or of different sizes. Guidance on what to do in the latter situation is found at RDA 3.5.2.3. If there are only two different sizes of sheets, record both sizes as shown below (see figure 4.10).

300   25 maps : $b color ; $c sheets 44 x 40 cm and 48 x 45 cm

But, if there are more than two sizes of sheets, in either direction, record the greatest height and the widest width followed by the phrase *or smaller* (see figure 4.11).

300   15 maps ; $c sheets 60 x 90 cm or smaller

If the sheets are meant to be fitted together to create one map or if the map is divided into segments, then consult RDA 3.5.2.4. Not surprisingly, give the dimensions of the map as if it were joined together as well as the dimensions of the sheets so that those searching for the map will know what they are looking for (see figure 4.12). Going back to the map of Chile, the full 300 field would be:

300   1 map in 3 segments : $b color ; $c 144 x 22 cm, on sheet 55 x 65 cm

EXAMPLE FOR MAP BELOW

300   1 map on 4 sheets : $b color ; $c 160 x 190 cm, on sheets 88 x 103 cm

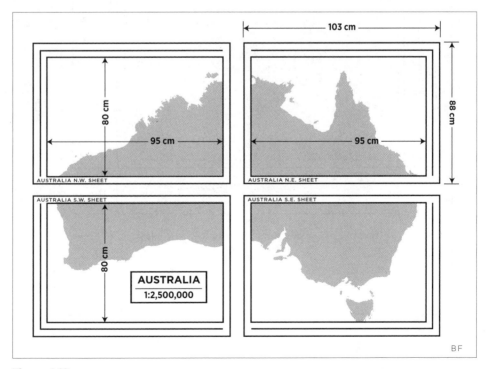

Figure 4.12
Map measurements example for one map on two or more sheets

If it is not possible to determine the size of the map when assembled, record only the size of the sheets as instructed in RDA 3.5.2.3.

RDA 3.5.2.5 covers what to do in those situations when the measurement of any dimension of the map is less than half of the same dimension of the sheet. Give the size of the map followed by the phrase "on sheet," and then give the sheet dimensions (see figure 4.13).

EXAMPLE

300   1 map : $b color ; $c 45 x 69 cm, on sheet 102 x 102 cm

Folded maps have traditionally been a major component of many map collections. Giving only the dimensions of the unfolded map in the bibliographic record could

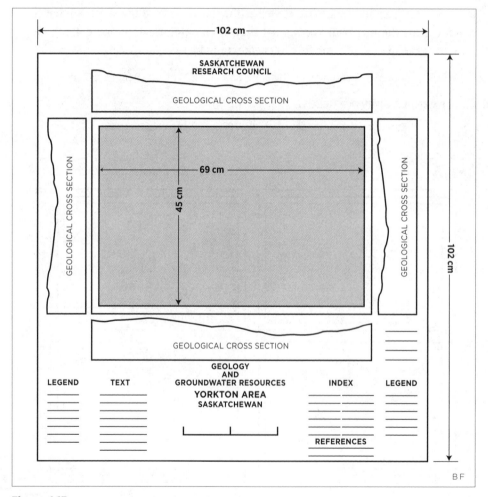

Figure 4.13
Map measurements example when one dimension of the map is less than half the same dimension of the sheet

mislead those looking for the map in the collection. According to RDA 3.5.2.6, the dimensions of the map are given, followed then by the dimensions of the folded sheet (see figure 4.14; this illustration shows a map folded into an exterior cover).

EXAMPLE

300 1 map : $b color ; $c 65 x 89 cm, folded in cover 18 x 23 cm

It is typical to find a map of this type also folded into what is known as a panel, which is part of the printed sheet. In such a case, it is also necessary to add the folded size to the end of the dimensions statement, as described above, though the phrase changes slightly to "folded to" to fit the circumstance.

EXAMPLE

300   1 map : $b both sides, color ; $c 85 x 52 cm, on sheet 46 x 67 cm, folded
       to 23 x 11 cm

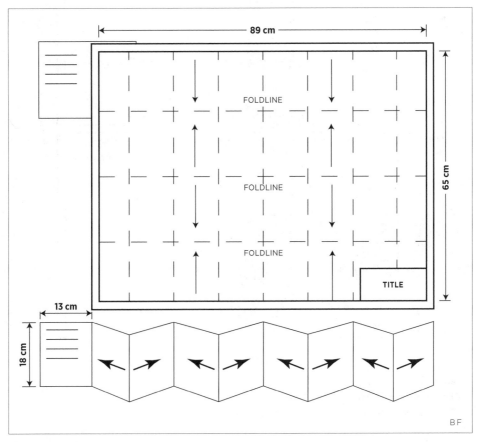

Figure 4.14
Map measurements example of a folded map

As noted in the section on layout earlier in this chapter, a single map can be printed on both sides of one sheet. RDA 3.5.2.7 instructs the cataloger to record the dimensions of the map as a whole and then follow that with the phrase "on sheet" and give the dimensions of the sheet (see figure 4.15). If determining the dimensions of the whole map is too difficult, just record the dimensions of the sheet.

EXAMPLE

300   1 map : $b both sides, color ; $c 85 x 52 cm, on sheet 46 x 67 cm

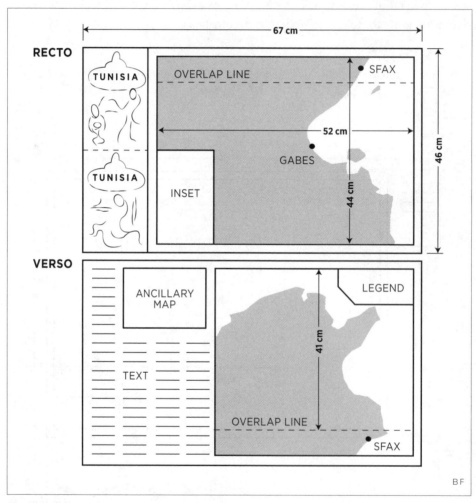

Figure 4.15
Map measurements example for one map that starts on one side
of the sheet and continues on the opposite side

300$e ACCOMPANYING MATERIAL

Maps occasionally come with resources that provide additional information about them. As with AACR2, RDA provides the option of either including the information about the accompanying material as part of the 300 field or as a note. First, determine what the resource as a whole is, following the instructions at RDA 2.1.2.3. Admittedly, the instructions in 2.1.2.3 are not helpful in this circumstance, but item "d" is the closest fit. In most instances for cartographic resources, the map is the primary resource and the text or other resource serves to augment the map. The clearest guidance for describing accompanying material is found at the LC-PCC PS for RDA 3.1.4, the authors recommend following 1b within the policy statement. Recording the physical description of the accompanying material follows the same guidelines as for the physical description of the primary resource. Using ISBD punctuation, the description of the accompanying material is set off by parentheses (see RDA D.1.2.6 for details).

EXAMPLE

300   1 map : $b both sides, color ; $c 97 x 46 cm, on sheet 50 x 56 cm + $e 1
        volume (ix, 120 pages : illustrations ; 28 cm)

If preferred, use the option of making a note about the accompanying material as indicated above. The instructions for doing so can be found at RDA 3.1.4, but the clearest instruction for this method is found at the LC-PCC PS for 3.1.4, notably item 3. Item 3 then refers the cataloger to specific note types depending on what is to be described; those are found at RDA 3.21.2 or 7.16.

If the accompanying material has a substantially different title than the material to which it relates, refer to RDA appendix J.2.5 for instructions on adding an optional relator field.

EXAMPLE

774 08 $i Guide to (work): $a Egorov, S.V. $t Explanatory notes for the International
        Hydrogeological Map of Europe, sheet E 3 Moskva.

336 CONTENT TYPE, 337 MEDIA TYPE, 338 CARRIER TYPE

Note that the 336, 337, and 338 fields are commonly described as the fields replacing the general material designation (GMD). They serve similar, but not identical, functions as the GMD. Because they are commonly referred to together, all three will be discussed in this section. Appendix E of this manual provides examples of the 336, 337, and 338 field combinations commonly used for cartographic resources.

The Library of Congress developed a set of terms and codes for each field that can be found in "Value Lists for Codes and Controlled Vocabularies" (www.loc.gov/standards/valuelist/). This Web page links to individual tables.

Based on online discussions, the disappearance of the GMD and the creation of the 33X fields seem to be one of the most "disruptive" aspects of RDA implementation. However, once an integrated library system is set up to handle the new fields, they are not that difficult to apply. An easy way to think about these fields is that the 336 Content type answers the question "what is it?," the 337 Media type answers "how is it stored?," and the 338 Carrier type answers "where is it stored?"

Background to Content Type

Content type

- is core (RDA 6.9)
- is one of the three fields commonly described as replacing the GMD

Content type is defined in RDA as "a categorization reflecting the fundamental form of communication in which the content is expressed and the human sense through which it is intended to be perceived." For images, this also reflects the number of dimensions in which the content is perceived as well as the perceived presence or absence of movement.

There are three subfields in the 336 that will be discussed here because they are the primary subfields used in cartographic resource cataloging. They are the $a for content type term, the $b for content type code, and the $2 for source. The instructions for the content type are at RDA 6.9.

336$a CONTENT TYPE TERM

RDA 6.9.1.3 instructs the cataloger to record the type of content contained in the resource using the terms provided, while using as many of the terms as needed to describe the resource adequately. The terms most commonly used for cartographic resources are "cartographic image," "cartographic moving image," "cartographic tactile image," "cartographic tactile three-dimensional form," "cartographic three-dimensional form," and "cartographic dataset." If none of these terms applies, use the term "other" or "unspecified." Note that in AACR2 "cartographic image" meant specifically a remote-sensing image, whereas RDA uses the term "image" in a much broader context. "Cartographic dataset" is for geographic information system/science datasets, and therefore is not the correct term for a scanned cartographic image or an image collected by a digital sensor. So for a single sheet map, the 336 field will show:

336   cartographic image

336$b CONTENT TYPE CODE

When the 33X fields were created for the MARC format, the developers thought that it would be a good option to allow for codes to be associated with the various terms used. Content type codes are listed in LC's *Term and Code List for RDA Content Types* (www.loc.gov/standards/valuelist/rdacarrier.html). (Note that the LC Geography and Map Division has chosen not use the $b for any of the 33X fields, and because the codes are optional some records will omit subfield "b.") For the single sheet map, the 336 field is now:

336   cartographic image $b cri

336$2 SOURCE

For all of the 33X fields, specify the source of the terms and codes used. Each 33X field has a slightly different source. For the 336 field, the source should always be "rdacontent," indicating that the term comes from the list provided at RDA 6.9.1.3 in table 6.1. So the full 336 field for a single sheet map is:

336   cartographic image $b cri $2 rdacontent

Background to Media Type

Media tye is

- not considered core in RDA (3.2)
- still commonly recorded in the bibliographic record

The instructions for recording media type are found at RDA 3.2.1.3. The 337 field differs from the 336 and 338 in that it is not considered a core element in RDA. However, this element is considered core in LC-PCC practice; therefore, this practice is followed here.

Media type is defined as a "categorization reflecting the general type of intermediation device required to view, play, run, etc., the content of the resource" in RDA 3.2.1.1. As such, it provides helpful information for users as it alerts them to possibly needing a device to view the resource(s).

As with the 336 field, there are three subfields that will be discussed here. They are the $a for media type term, the $b for media type code, and the $2 for source.

337$a MEDIA TYPE TERM

RDA 3.2.1.3 tells us to record the media type using one or more terms from its table 3.1. The list of terms for media type is much shorter than the list for content type. For cartographic resources, the terms most commonly used are "unmediated," "computer," "microform," and "stereographic." Again, if none of these terms applies, apply the term "other." Returning to the single sheet map, the 337 field will start with:

337   unmediated

337$b MEDIA TYPE CODE

For the same reason as for the content type, there are codes for the 337$b. The table of codes can be found at the *Term and Code List for RDA Media Types*. Checking for the code for "unmediated" in the code list, the 337 field now looks like this:

337   unmediated $b n

337$2 SOURCE

Again, as with the 336 field, indicate the source of the terms and codes used in the 337 field. For all the terms taken from RDA table 3.1, the source code will be "rdamedia." Therefore the completed 337 field for a single sheet map is:

337   unmediated $b n $2 rdamedia

Background to Carrier Type

Carrier type

- is core in RDA (RDA 3.3)
- is the last of the fields considered replacing the GMD

The instructions for recording carrier type are found at RDA 3.3. Carrier type is defined as the "categorization reflecting the format of the storage medium and housing of a carrier in combination with the type of intermediation device required to view, play, run, etc., the content of a resource."

Once again, there are three subfields that will be discussed here. They are carrier type term in $a, carrier type code in $b, and source in $2.

338$a CARRIER TYPE TERM

Use the terms provided at RDA 3.3.1.3. Unlike the 336 and 337 fields, the terms are given in a list rather than a table. However, if none of the terms is appropriate, once again use the term "other." The most common terms used for cartographic resources are "sheet," "object," "online resource," and "microfiche," although others may apply. Turning once again to the single sheet map, the 338 field starts out as:

338   sheet

338$b CARRIER TYPE CODE

Checking the code for "sheet" in the *Term and Code List for RDA Carrier Types* shows that it is "nb." So the 338 field now looks like this:

    338   sheet $b nb

338$2 SOURCE

Again, record the source of the term used in this field. The source code for terms taken from RDA 3.3.1.3 is "rdacarrier." So the completed 338 field for a single sheet map is:

    338   sheet $b nb $2 rdacarrier

Remember that the $b subfields are not used by the Library of Congress Geography and Map Division, so if the decision is made to follow their practice these codes will not appear in the record.

For other common 336, 337, 338 combinations based on a given resource refer to appendix E in this manual.

5XX NOTE FIELDS UNIQUE OR COMMON TO CARTOGRAPHIC RESOURCES

While catalogers are able to supply various kinds of notes to bring out specific bits of data not found elsewhere in the bibliographic record description, or, just as importantly, to elucidate and describe data found elsewhere, there are several notes that are either unique to, or most commonly used for, cartographic resources. In addition, catalogers will find that because cartographic resources are graphic in nature, they typically employ many more notes than would be used, for example, with monographs.

Remember that RDA is focused on relationships, and this is no different when it comes to notes. Notes can be described in two different ways in RDA: first by their relationship level within the WEMI model, and then second (as with AACR2) by the type of note. In the first instance certain notes apply to expression-level data, others to manifestation-level data, still others to item-level data. Examples specific to cartographic resources follow.

Expression-Level Note

    500   Primary scale of resource is 1:50,000.

This would be an instance where the cataloger chose to use the standard phrase "Scales differ" for several main maps in a set or atlas with different scales, using RDA 7.25.1.4.

Manifestation-Level Note

500   Title from panel. (See RDA 20.2.3.)

Item-Level Note

590   Local copy sheet size is 101 x 168 cm. (See RDA 2.19.)

Identifying notes by their "type" or by what they are describing from or about the resource is easily recognizable from AACR2 days. Common note types are those such as:

- "Nature and scope of item" notes that begin with "Shows . . ." or "Relief shown by . . ."
- "Statement of responsibility" notes for identifying those persons and/or bodies not named in the MARC 245$c Statement of Responsibility element
- "Mathematical and other material specific details" notes, such as those identifying prime meridians that are not the Greenwich prime meridian, e.g., Ferro or Paris

as are contents notes. These in turn lend themselves to a particular order in the record as well.

Before delving into categorizing and then laying out the kinds of notes map catalogers are used to providing, it is worth sharing that RDA 1.10 provides a high-level view of what notes are and how to proceed in somewhat sticky situations:

> When the instructions in chapters 2–7 specify making a note, apply the following general guidelines:
>
> capitalization (see 1.10.2)
> quotations (see 1.10.3)
> references (see 1.10.4)
> applicability of the information recorded in a note (see 1.10.5).

For cartographic resources, the first two of these are straightforward, the third would likely not be used except with historical cartographic resources, and the fourth is very useful because it shares data that might only apply to a single main map when multiple main maps are described elsewhere in the record. It would be worth reviewing each of these instructions when learning to apply various notes.

The following categories of notes can be described as either "essential" or "helpful additional information." The majority of categories are covered by instructions found in RDA chapters 2 and 3, but a couple of specific kinds are found in RDA chapters 5 and 7 because they relate to expressions, as highlighted above. No matter which of the WEMI levels a note belongs to, the important point is to provide information within notes that assists the user in understanding aspects of the cartographic resource being described.

Examples of Essential Cartographic Notes

Maps often display unique categories of information that require specific notes to make users aware of their presence, as well as to help catalogers in determining how to match bibliographic copy. The following categories of information, if present on the resource, should always be brought out in the bibliographic record in the form of MARC 500 general notes:

A. Elevation (Relief) and/or Depth

EXAMPLES

Relief shown by contours and spot heights.
Relief shown by spot heights.
Depths shown by soundings.
Depths shown by bathymetric isolines and soundings.

B. Source of Title If Not Found with the Map Itself, or "Within the Neat Line"

EXAMPLES

Title from panel. (or Title from cover.)
Title from accompanying text.
Folded title. (earlier form of the note.)

C. Orientation (When "North" Is not Pointing "Up" on the Map)

EXAMPLES

Oriented with north to the upper left.
Oriented with north to the right.

D. Unique Mathematical Data

EXAMPLES

Prime meridian: Washington D.C.
"Origin of revenue survey coordinates, Lat. 20°43'15", Long. 101°56'36"."

E. Information Regarding Dates of Publication or Situation

EXAMPLES

"Effective date: July 17, 1987."
"Surveys by Norges Svalbard- og Ishavs-Undersokelser, 1909-1939."

F. Physical Description

EXAMPLES

Geographic coverage complete in 12 sheets.

Originally issued in a cover.

G. Unique Numbering/Alphanumeric Designation(s)

EXAMPLES

"10869."

"Base 881369 (R46079) 7-97."

Additional Note Types for Clarification and/or Further Information

A. Other Statements of Responsibility Not Found in the MARC 245$c
    Subfield

EXAMPLES

"Base compiled from latest USGS quad sheets."

"Copyright ... Rand McNally."

Stamped on: Library of Congress, two copies received Jun 1 1904, copyright entry
May 7 1904, Class E, XXc No. 5663, copy A.

B. "Includes" Notes

EXAMPLES

Includes text, street index, and inset of downtown area.

Includes list of area attractions, notes, church services schedule, advertisements, and
color illustration.

C. "On Verso" Notes

EXAMPLE

Directory of tourist locations, text, and color illustrations on verso.

D. Accompanying Material (if Not Covered in 300$e)

EXAMPLES

Accompanied by: Nouveau plan d'Elizabethville. (6 pages ; 24 cm).

Accompanies thesis: Geology of a portion of the Allensville 15′ quadrangle, Pennsylvania, call number Thesis 1967m Fleuc, L.A.

E. Language(s) (Use the MARC 546 Field)

EXAMPLE

Place names in Dutch. Cover in English. Legend and tourist directory
in Dutch, French, German, and English.

CONTENT NOTES

Content notes, or those placed in a MARC 505 field, are not unique to cartographic
resources, but are used regularly in describing them and are very helpful to users and
catalogers for identification purposes. Additionally, if the field is indexed for keyword
searching capability, the ability to expand retrieved results is enhanced from the data
provided in this particular field.

Cartographic resources content notes are employed under two primary circumstances: when the resource includes more than one main map on a single sheet, or
when main maps appear across multiple physical sheets or other carriers. Most often
the case encountered is when there are multiple main maps on a single carrier (sheet)
and the title in the 245 field is representative of all, such as:

245 10 Motor vehicle use map, Kiowa and Rita Blanca National grasslands, Cibola
         National Forest, NM, TX, OK ...

505 0   Map 1 of 2. Kiowa National Grassland, Mills Unit -- Map 2 of 2. Kiowa National
         Grassland [and] Rita Blanca National Grassland.

In the case below, the two main maps appear on two separate sheets under one
collective title:

505 0   Plate 3-A. Primary influences in the study area, urban portion -- Plate 3-A.
         Primary influences in the study area, rural portion.

Using cataloger's judgment, the cataloger may also wish to bring out specific cartographic resources within an atlas because of the generic nature of the title proper,
whereas the titles of the individual resources within are very specific. For example:

245 10 Geophysical series. $p NTS 64-I/09 and part of NTS 54 L/12 : $b Airborne
         geophysical survey of the Great Island and Seal River area, Manitoba ...

505 0   [1] Natural air absorbed dose rate = Taux d'absorption naturel des rayons
         gamma dans l'air -- [2] Potassium -- [3] Uranium -- [4] Thorium -- [5]
         Uranium/Thorium -- [6] Uranium/Potassium -- [7] Thorium/Potassium -- [8]
         Ternary radioelement map.

Finally, another common technique in terms of sharing multiples of content, such as when numerous inset maps or ancillary maps are included in the resource, is to do a "contents-like" note using a 500 field, such as:

> 500   Insets: Fox Valley -- Munds Park -- Hart Prairie -- Blue Ridge -- Munds Park -- Fossil Creek.

Note for Original Version Data and Using Linking Data for Cartographic Resources Reproductions

The topic of cartographic facsimiles was raised in chapter 3 as part of the general discussion of the treatment of facsimiles in RDA. Map catalogers have long recorded data elements about the facsimile in hand, but data about the original resource, if known, were recorded in a MARC 534 original version note. The last part of the OCLC definition of the field, "Use field 534 when details relevant to the original differ from the information describing the reproduction," describes what is being done. While the continued use of the 534 field remains acceptable for hardcopy resources, it is now very common to scan a paper map, creating a digital cartographic resource. Thus, catalogers must look to using MARC linking entry fields, the 775 or 776. In fact, for LC and PCC catalogers, related manifestation data are considered a core element, and a very good explanation for including such data is found at the LC-PCC PS for RDA 27.1.

How to apply these two fields––the 775 and 776––appears in the LC-PCC PS for RDA 27.1.1.3, which explicitly states that the guidelines for these fields are "LC/PCC practice." The policy statement guidelines for are below, with the *OCLC Bibliographic Formats and Standards* field definitions embedded after each policy statement quoted:

1. USING MARC FIELD 775

> Relationship to the original: on the record for the reproduction, use a structured description to give the attributes of the original.
>
> a) Carrier of reproduction is the same as the carrier of the original:
>   use MARC field 775.

The MARC 775 Other Edition Entry field is defined in OCLC as including "information about the other available editions in a horizontal relationship with the work" and provides three different circumstances. The third of these, "other editions," is for "other editions of the target item. These editions will generally bear the same title as the target item, but have edition information that distinguishes them" (OCLC 2013).

2. USING MARC FIELD 776

Relationship to the original: on the record for the reproduction, use a structured description to give the attributes of the original.

b) When the carrier of reproduction is not the same as the carrier of the original: use MARC field 776.

The MARC 776 Additional Physical Form field is defined in OCLC as including "information about the other available physical forms of the target item in a horizontal relationship" (OCLC 2013). Use the relationship designator "Reproduction of (manifestation)" unless a particular PCC program (e.g., CONSER) recommends the use of a different relationship designator.

Therefore, if describing a facsimile on paper reproduced from an original on paper (see a. above), and data for the original exists, use the 775 field. The 776 field should be used in circumstances when the reproduction has a different carrier from the original, such as a map on microfiche produced from an original on paper, or most commonly, a digital version of a paper map. In both cases begin the field with "Reproduction of (manifestation)." Examples for both situations are provided in appendix G; see the records for a facsimile map and a map on microfiche.

Notes Related to Digital Cartographic Resources

Digital cartographic resources provide several kinds of information related to their electronic and/or online characteristics. When available, these pieces of data should be captured in notes designed to share just this kind of information. Most of the instructions relating to digital aspects of resources are found in two instructions: RDA 3.19, which discusses digital file characteristics, and 3.20, which discusses equipment or system requirements. (There is a helpful crosswalk table between RDA instruction number and MARC field number for elements in appendix F of this manual.) When it is time to record one or more of these characteristics, RDA allows ample room for cataloger's judgment: "Record digital file characteristics if considered important for identification or selection."

The LC-PCC PS for RDA 3.19 states that a "digital file characteristic is a core element for LC for cartographic resources." The authors recommend following this policy statement. For digital file characteristics sources of information, see RDA 3.19.1.2: "Use evidence presented by the resource itself (or on any accompanying material or container) as the basis for recording the digital file characteristics of the resource. Take additional evidence from any source."

We are fortunate that RDA established a specific set of digital elements instructions for cartographic resources, found at RDA 3.19.8. At RDA 3.19.8.3 the instruction outlines three elements to be recorded: data type (i.e., raster, vector, or point), object type (i.e., point, line, polygon, pixel), and number of objects used to represent spatial information. This data would appear in a MARC 352 field. Examples of instructions for other digital characteristics that can be recorded include RDA 3.19.4 for file size (MARC 347$c) and RDA 3.19.5 for resolution (MARC 347$d), among others.

Data falling under RDA 3.20 are familiar from AACR2, such as the "system requirement" notes typically found in the MARC 538 field.

Application of this suite of notes primarily falls under cataloger's judgment, though every attempt should be made to record information that will be helpful to the users of digital cartographic resources. After all, doing so fulfills the FRBR requirements of find, identify, select, and obtain, and digital resources gain importance through their use in our online environments.

REFERENCES

Cartographic Materials: A Manual of Interpretation for AACR2, 2002 Revision, Second Edition, 2003. Edited by Elizabeth Mangan. Chicago: American Library Association.

Joint Steering Committee for the Development of RDA. "Revision of 9.8.1.3, 9.9.1.3, 9.10.1.3, 9.11.1.3, 10.5.1.3, 11.3.1.3, 11.13.1.3, 16.2.2.4, 16.2.2.9.2, B.1, B.11 to eliminate use of abbreviations for places. British Library Follow up." February 21, 2014. www.rda-jsc.org/docs/6JSC-BL-10-BL-follow-up.pdf.

Klokan Technologies. 2012. Klokan Bounding Box Tool. http://boundingbox.klokantech.com/.

Library of Congress. Network Development and MARC Standards Office. Term and Code List for RDA Carrier Types. www.loc.gov/standards/valuelist/rdacarrier.html.

———. Term and Code List for RDA Content Types. www.loc.gov/standards/valuelist/.

———. Term and Code list for RDA Media Types. www.loc.gov/standards/valuelist/rdamedia.html.

———. Value Lists for Codes and Controlled Vocabularies. www.loc.gov/standards/valuelist.

Mazzone, Jason. 2006. "Copyfraud." *New York University Law Review* 81: 1026.

Moore, Susan. 2013. "How to Use the Natural Scale Indicator." YouTube video. www.youtube.com/watch?v=vSus_5bt440.

National Geospatial-Intelligence Agency. NGA GEOnet Names Server (GNS). http://earth-info.nga.mil/gns/html/index.html.

OCLC. 2013. *Bibliographic Formats and Standards.* 4th ed. www.oclc.org/bibformats/en.html.

USNO Geological Survey. Geographic Names Information System (GNIS). http://geonames.usgs.gov/pls/gnispublic/f?p=132:1:3695645352446379.

Western Association of Map Libraries. Map Librarian's Toolbox. www.waml.org/maptools.html.

CHAPTER 5

CARTOGRAPHIC RESOURCES CATALOGING

Moving Forward

WE HAVE REACHED THE END OF THIS TOUR OF HOW TO USE RDA TO catalog cartographic resources. As has been mentioned and demonstrated in previous chapters, the differences between using RDA to describe resources and using AACR2 to do that work are primarily in the details. The basic ideas of bibliographic description, such as providing a title, identifying who is responsible for creating the resource, and sharing physical attributes remain much the same. Catalogers who adapt to RDA are well prepared to adapt to future cataloging-code changes and to changes in any new standard to be developed for the delivery of bibliographic data. While fitting cartographic resources into the complete WEMI model is difficult, they fit most neatly at the expression and manifestation levels. Whereas the WEMI model works nearly perfectly with classical music, it is far from perfect for maps and other cartographic resources. Such are the limitations of a conceptual model.

Moving to RDA does require making changes to all cataloging manuals based on AACR2 rules, most notably for the MARC 255 and 300 fields, and is best done before implementation begins. There is no question that a considerable investment in time is required to update procedural manuals and create new documentation, and for training. Catalogers should be prepared for an increase in the length of time required to create each bibliographic record until they acquire enough experience using RDA to come up to speed. Anecdotal evidence from catalogers whose libraries have made the transition finds that they return to their AACR2 cataloging time-per-record after an adjustment period.

Implementing new MARC fields seems to be a process that integrated library system vendors deal with relatively quickly after OCLC has added them to its system. Locally, however, implementation of these new fields, including decisions about making the content of specific fields visible to the public using the online catalog versus only to library staff, must be made in partnership with map collection curators and library technical staff.

ADVANTAGES OF AACR2

AACR2 is a well-used, well-documented, and well-known, and therefore comfortable, standard that has been around since its implementation on January 1, 1981. Humans may prefer constant change but only in very small amounts. A change in cataloging codes—even if most of the change is in the details—does not qualify as a small change. An underlying primary challenge for catalogers is to learn the major theoretical principles underpinning RDA and its effect on the presentation of cataloging information. AACR2 rules are segregated by format for the eight different formats involved, which makes it easy to comprehend. In AACR2, a separate section includes rules covering access points. RDA instructions are organized quite differently.

Cataloging cartographic resources with AACR2 is relatively simple in that the cataloger uses its chapter 3 a very large percentage of the time, and refers to other chapters such as those for computer resources or serials less frequently. This one- or two-step process makes cataloging a single resource a relatively speedy procedure. RDA is arranged in a completely different manner—with instructions presented (and stated very generally) as to whether what is being cataloged is a work, an expression, a manifestation or an item. This means that there is a certain amount of leapfrogging around in RDA, whether using the print version or the online RDA Toolkit. While hyperlinks to other needed instructions ameliorate the situation, there are smaller libraries that might only be able to afford to use the hardcopy version of RDA. It is a horse of a different color when there is no access to those hyperlinks. AACR2 focuses on the resource in hand (the "item," in AACR2 parlance) and its complete description as a bibliographic record, with the item in hand representing all items for any one manifestation. In contrast, RDA more broadly focuses on the WEMI model's relationships and more narrowly focuses on the data element level.

DISADVANTAGES OF AACR2

Records created using AACR2 rules are generally not interoperable with other kinds of data records or metadata schema without the help of a crosswalk and related tools. Other interoperability issues deal with various problems such as different records not having exact field-level matches, fields of importance in one standard not necessarily having a related field even similar to them in another standard, and so forth. However, RDA was created for, and is intended to be used with, a multiplicity of standards, for example those dealing with any type of bibliographic or archival metadata.

ADVANTAGES OF RDA

Because relationships are at the center of the FRBR model around which RDA is structured, it is easier to bring together in a meaningful way those things related to, and related within, a given resource—whether due to changes in expression and/or manifestation or by a better way of showing how works, expressions, and manifestations are interrelated. Provided that a specific library's decisions allow for necessary configurations of indexed—and therefore retrievable—data, and also options taken regarding display choices, the patron's ability to understand and access records will be improved.

Seemingly minor changes that are of great importance for improving user comprehension include using abbreviations sparingly, and never using Latin terms—especially not in their abbreviated form. It would help users considerably if the change in abbreviation practices were extended to subject headings so that, for example, there would be no abbreviations of names of states in the United States (a change being considered by the Joint Steering Committee for RDA). Under current subject-creation rules, when providing a subject heading that begins with a geographic name the name of the larger geographic area of which it is a part is abbreviated:

> Santa Barbara (Calif.) $v Maps.

On the other hand, if the resource is thematic in nature, the topic or subject word (topical heading) appears first and then the geographic name appears in its full, spelled-out-but-inverted form:

> Geology $z California $z Santa Barbara $v Maps.

Any librarian who has ever worked at a reference desk knows well the futility of attempting to explain these subtleties to users searching a library's online system. Although these structures worked well when users were dealing with a traditional card catalog, very few libraries live in that world now.

DISADVANTAGES OF RDA

In the short run, there is a long learning curve for the cataloger that must begin with understanding the theoretical underpinnings of RDA, most notably FRBR (using several models such as WEMI), and how inherent relationships are expressed.

Additionally, at the time of publication there is a lack of format-specific documentation for guidance, which compels catalogers to wend their way through the instructions as best they can, and to discuss application issues with fellow catalogers. Finally, the RDA Toolkit is not an intuitive online tool for most catalogers accustomed to AACR2, and thus has its own separate learning curve.

POSTSCRIPT

THIS BOOK HAS REVIEWED THE PHILOSOPHICAL UNDERPINNINGS OF RDA, explored the major and subtle differences between AACR2 and RDA, and provided some examples of what the two standards have in common, as well as in how they differ. While one book cannot provide all the answers to every situation encountered when describing cartographic resources, the authors' major goal is to help catalogers get started down the RDA path. As was the case with AACR2, there will continue to be refinements and interpretations to the RDA instructions, possibly driving the creation of new or revised documentation such as this manual. The authors hope that this book provides catalogers a solid base from which to continue to explore and deal with whatever comes next, whether it be changes to RDA or eventually a new cataloging standard.

IMAGE OF
DAMIETTA SHEET
FROM THE EGYPT
1:100,000 SERIES

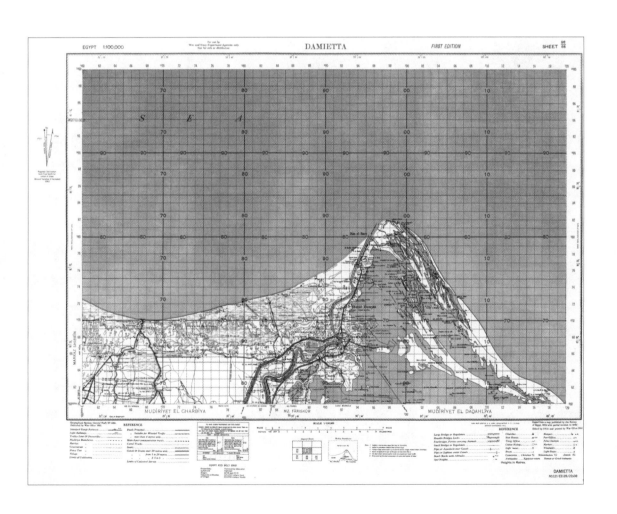

MAP RECORD EXAMPLE SHOWING FRBR RELATIONSHIP ENTITIES INVOLVED AT THE FIELD LEVEL

007		a $b j $d c $e a $f n $g z $h n
040		UPM $b eng $e rda $c UPM
034	1	a $b 5500000 $d E0340000 $e E0620000 $f N0320000 $g N0120000
042		pcc
050	4	G7521.H8 1957 $b .A8 *Call number as a whole = Item; Class number alone = Work*
052		7521
049		UPMM
245	00	Arabian Peninsula, petroleum concessions, oil fields, and installations, Jan. 1957 : $b concession area ownership including offshore concessions. → *Manifestation entity*
250		First revised 2-57. → *Manifestation entity*
255		Scale approximately 1:5,500,000 $c (E 34°--E 62°/N 32°--N 12°). → *Scale statement = Expression; Coordinates statement = Work*
264	1	[Washington, D.C.] : $b [U.S. Department of State?,] $c [1957] → *Manifestation entity*
300		1 map : $b color ; $c 41 x 47 cm → *Manifestation entity except for "color" = Expression*
336		cartographic image $b cri $2 rdacontent → *Expression entity*
337		unmediated $b n $2 rdamedia → *Manifestation entity*
338		sheet $b nb $2 rdacarrier → *Manifestation entity*

500   Includes table with an index of "Operating Companies" and their "Controlling Interests", and additional legend for boundaries. → *Manifestation entity*

500   "25338 3-56 (First Revision 2-57)." → *Manifestation entity*

500   "SSO -- 176-2/57." → *Manifestation entity*

650   0 Petroleum $z Arabian Peninsula $v Maps. → *Subject heading and subdivision = Work; $v genre/form heading = Expression*

650   0 Petroleum pipelines $z Arabian Peninsula $v Maps. → *same as above*

650 0   Petroleum refineries $z Arabian Peninsula $v Maps. → *same as above*

650 0   Petroleum industry and trade $z Arabian Peninsula $v Maps. → *same as above*

655 7   Thematic maps. $2 lcgft → *Expression entity*

710 1   United States. $b Department of State. → *Work entity*

RDA CHECKLIST FOR DESCRIPTIVE ELEMENTS

From the Pennsylvannia State University Maps Cataloging Team's Web page on documentation (www.libraries.psu.edu/psul/cataloging/maps/docs/rdachecklist.html).

General

"Take what you see"—record fully and exactly all transcription fields or subfields (e.g., 245, 250, 255$b, 264)

Don't abbreviate, unless abbreviated on the item; exceptions include "in." for inch/inches and "ft." for foot/feet (see RDA appendix B, table at B.7)

Don't use Latin phrases such as "sic," "et al.," or "S.l." and "s.n."

FIXED FIELD

Desc: Should be coded "i"

VARIABLE FIELDS

040 Add "$b eng $e rda" after initial subfield $a and before $c (if the workform in OCLC Connexion is set to the RDA template the $e rda will already be in the field as system-supplied data, so only the $b code "eng" will need to be added)

1XX   Creators must get $e relationship designator if one can be determined; most commonly this will be "cartographer" but could be something like "compiler" or "publisher"

245   Transcribe subfields $a, $b, and $c exactly

In $c, for multiple creators performing the same function, add the first as required because it is core; add others as desired (cataloger's judgment)

255   Use "Scale approximately 1:___" for derived scale (No more "ca." and no more brackets)

264   Use 264 in place of 260; second indicator 1 equals Publication function/role; other Indicator values equal different functions/roles

Bracket supplied data; bracket each subfield *individually*

Do not use [S.l.] or [s.n.]—use [place of publication unknown] and [publisher unknown] *if neither a place of publication and/or publisher can be determined by other means*

When deriving publication date from copyright date, bracket date without the letter "c" designation

When copyright date is available and is either the same as, or different from, publication date, record it separately in a second 264 with indicator value of 4 [i.e., "264 _4"]

Use [date of publication unknown] if there is no means to identify one from any source

300   Be careful to spell out elements such as "color," "manuscript," etc.

"cm" is a symbol, and should not have a period associated with it

This field only ends in a period when there is a 4XX statement following it

For a sheet map, as but one example:

336   cartographic image $2 rdacontent

337   unmediated $2 rdamedia

338   sheet $2 rdacarrier

7XX   Added entries may receive a subfield $e relationship designator (cataloger's judgment except for first named creator)

EXAMPLES OF CORRECT SCALE AND COORDINATES NOTATION IN THE 255 FIELD WITH MATCHING EXAMPLES IN THE 034 FIELD UNDER AACR2 AND RDA

Note: when inputting coordinates into the record being created in OCLC use the *degree symbol* for degrees, *miagkii znak* for minutes, and *tverdyi znak* for seconds, as found in the "ALA Characters" box, when using that method.

Two general rules of thumb to follow:

1. Order of degrees, minutes, and seconds must be consistent across subfield "c" in the 255
2. Numbers must match between scale/coordinates given in the 255 and those given in 034

034 1   a $b 55000
255   Scale [ca. 1:55,000].
RDA = Scale approximately 1:55,000.

(Note: do *not* use a comma in the 034 field, subfield "b")

034 1   a $b 1000000 $d W1250000 $e W0650000 $f N0500000 $g N0250000
255   Scale 1:1,000,000 $c (W 125°--W 65°/N 50°--N 25°).

a. Note: **subfield "c"** is used only for vertical scale in the 034 field

b. Note: **no punctuation** is used between the end of the scale statement (subfield "a") and the beginning of subfield "c" in the 255 field, with two exceptions (see end of this appendix).

RDA = Scale 1:1,000,000 $c (W 125°--W 65°/N 50°--N 25°).

034 1   a $b 250000 $d W0063000 $e E0101500 $f N0280000 $g N0174500
255   Scale 1:250,000 $c (W 6°30'--E 10°15'/N 28°00'--N 17°45').

RDA = Scale 1:250,000 $c (W 6°30'--E 10°15'/N 28°00'--N 17°45').

034 1   a $b 100000 $d E0154730 $e E0381000 $f S0055510 $g S0352249
255   Scale ca. 1:100,000 $c (E 15°47'30"--E 38°10'00"/S 5°55'10"--S 35°22'49").

RDA = Scale approximately 1:100,000 $c (E 15°47'30"--E 38°10'00"/S 5°55'10"--S 35°22'49").

NOT:

255   Scale 1:50,000 $c (W 82°30'--W 76°/N 33°20'05"--N 30°10').

034 0 a   034 0 a   034 0 a   034 0 a
255   Scales differ. 255   Scale not given. 255   Not drawn to scale. 255   Scale varies.

FINALLY: The only two times that punctuation is used between the end of the scale statement and the beginning of subfield "c" in the 255 field is: a period immediately following the scale statement and before wording of an equivalent scale statement or other wording is given, and/or a semicolon following the scale statement but before a statement of projection. Examples follow:

255   Scale [1:744,080]. 1 in. = 28 miles ; $b transverse Mercator proj.
RDA = Scale 1:744,080. 1 in. = 28 miles ; $b transverse Mercator projection

255   Scale 1:10,000 ; $b polyconic proj. $c (W 55°--W 48°/N 48°--N 32°).
RDA = Scale 1:10,000 ; $b polyconic projection $c (W 55°--W 48°/N 48°--N 32°).

33X CONTENT, MEDIA, AND CARRIER TERMS EXAMPLES BASED ON DIFFERENT KINDS OF CARTOGRAPHIC RESOURCES

Non-Digital Resources

SHEET MAP (SINGLE SHEET) ON PAPER OR SIMILAR

336 cartographic image $b cri $2 rdacontent
337 unmediated $b n $2 rdamedia
338 sheet $b nb $2 rdacarrier

SHEET MAP (MULTIPLE SHEETS, EITHER 1 MAP ON X SHEETS OR MAP SET/SERIES) ON PAPER OR SIMILAR

336 cartographic image $b cri $2 rdacontent
337 unmediated $b n $2 rdamedia
338 sheet $b nb $2 rdacarrier

ATLAS IN HARDCOPY FORM

336 cartographic image $b cri $2 rdacontent
337 unmediated $b n $2 rdamedia
338 volume $b nc $2 rdacarrier
    or

336 cartographic image $b cri $2 rdacontent
336 text $b txt $c rdacontent
337 unmediated $b n $2 rdamedia
338 volume $b nc $2 rdacarrier

GLOBE

336 cartographic three-dimensional form $b crf $2 rdacontent
337 unmediated $b n $2 rdamedia
338 object $b nr $2 rdacarrier

MAP ON MICROFICHE

336 cartographic image $b cri $2 rdacontent
337 microform $b h $2 rdamedia
338 microfiche $b he $2 rdacarrier

REMOTE-SENSING IMAGES

336 cartographic image $b cri $2 rdacontent
337 unmediated $b n $2 rdamedia
338 sheet $b nb $2 rdacarrier

RAISED-RELIEF MODEL

336 cartographic three-dimensional form $b crf $2 rdacontent
337 unmediated $b n $2 rdamedia
338 sheet $b nb $2 rdacarrier

Tactile Non-Digital Resources

SHEET MAP

336 cartographic tactile image $b crt $2 rdacontent
337 unmediated $b n $2 rdamedia
338 sheet $b nb $2 rdacarrier

ATLAS

336 cartographic tactile image $b cri $2 rdacontent
337 unmediated $b n $2 rdamedia
338 volume $b nc $2 rdacarrier

GLOBE

336 cartographic tactile three-dimensional form $b crn $2 rdacontent
337 unmediated $b n $2 rdamedia
338 object $b nr $2 rdacarrier

Digital Resources (CD-ROM or Similar)

MAP

336 cartographic image $b cri $2 rdacontent
337 computer $b c $2 rdamedia
338 computer disc $b cd $2 rdacarrier

ATLAS

336 cartographic image $b cri $2 rdacontent
337 computer $b c $2 rdamedia
338 computer disc $b cd $2 rdacarrier

REMOTE-SENSING IMAGES

336 cartographic image $b cri $2 rdacontent
337 computer $b c $2 rdamedia
338 computer disc $b cd $2 rdacarrier

Online Resources

MAP

336 cartographic image $b cri $2 rdacontent
337 computer $b c $2 rdamedia
338 online resource $b cr $2 rdacarrier

ATLAS

336 cartographic image $b cri $2 rdacontent
337 computer $b c $2 rdamedia
338 online resource $b cr $2 rdacarrier

REMOTE-SENSING IMAGES

336 cartographic image $b cri $2 rdacontent
337 computer $b c $2 rdamedia
338 online resource $b cr $2 rdacarrier

DIGITAL RESOURCES NOTES
Comparing RDA Number
with MARC Field Number

RDA #	Name of Instruction or MARC Field	MARC Field #
3.19.1	Digital File Characteristics	347
3.19.2	File Type	516 or 347 $a
3.19.3	Encoding Format	300 $b or 347 $b
3.19.4	File Size	300 $a or 347 $c
3.19.5	Resolution	347 $d
3.19.8	Digital Representation of Cartographic Content	352
N/A	Data Quality Note	514
3.19.3 and 3.20	System Details	538
N/A	Entity/Attribute Information	552
3.19.8.4	Geospatial Reference Data	342
N/A [data on co-ordinates is found at 7.4; planar, or *x,y* coordinates are not covered]	Planar Coordinates Data	343

SAMPLE RECORDS FOR DIFFERENT CARTOGRAPHIC RESOURCE TYPES

Record for a Single Map on One Side of Sheet

007	a $b j $d c $e a $f n $g z $h n
040	UPM $b eng $e rda $c UPM
034 1	a $b 88000 $d W0745900 $e W0741700 $f N0413000 $g N0405000
052	3813 $b S9
090	G3813.S9 1955 $b .H3
049	UPMM
100 1	Harper, George B., $e cartographer.
245 10	Sussex County, New Jersey / $c corrected to 1955 by George B. Harper, County Engineer.
255	Scale approximately 1:88,000 $c (W 74°59'--W 74°17'/N 41°30'--N 40°50').
264 1	Convent Station, N.J. : $b General Drafting Co., Inc., $c [1955]
300	1 map : $b color ; $c 62 x 59 cm, folded to 22 x 10 cm
336	cartographic image $b cri $2 rdacontent
337	unmediated $b n $2 rdamedia
338	sheet $b nb $2 rdacarrier
500	"All borough streets are improved."
500	Includes a location map and two illustrations.

500   Text, illustrations with captions, and mailing area on verso.

651 0 Sussex County (N.J.) $v Maps.

655 7 Maps. $2 lcgft

710 2 General Drafting Company.

Record for a Remote-Sensing Image

007   a $b r $d a $e a $f n $g z $h n

040   UPM $b eng $e rda $c UPM $d OCLCQ $d UPM $d OCLCQ

034 0 a $d W0773000 $e W0753000 $f N0410000 $g N0393000

042   pcc

043   n-us-pa

050 4 G3792.S9A43 1975 $b .E7

052   3792 $b S9 $b D44

052   3821

049   UPMM

110 2 EROS Data Center.

245 10 [Satellite image of the Susquehanna River Valley and watershed in Pennsylvania, including portions of northernmost Chesapeake Bay and Delaware Bay and southernmost portion of the Delaware River]. $n E-2112-15072-5-01.

255   Scale not given $c (W 77°30′--W 75°30′/N 41°00′--N 39°30′).

264 1 [Sioux Falls, S.D.] : $b National Aeronautics and Space Administration, $c 1975.

300   1 remote-sensing image ; $c 36 x 39 cm, on sheet 46 x 51 cm

336   cartographic image $b cri $2 rdacontent

337   unmediated $b n $2 rdamedia

338   sheet $b nb $2 rdacarrier

522   Shows the Susquehanna River valley and watershed from approximately Lewisburg, Pennsylvania down to the northern reaches of Chesapeake Bay where the river and bay confluence. Also shows the Delaware River where it flows into northern Delaware Bay near Wilmington, Delaware.

500   Title devised by cataloger.

500   "14MAY75."

500   Glossy monochrome photograph on Kodak paper.

500   "C N40-08/W076-21 N N40-08/W076-17 MSS 5 D SUN EL57 AZ122 191-1560-N-I-N-D-2L NASA ERTS."

651 0 Susquehanna River Watershed $v Remote-sensing images.

651 0 Delaware River (N.Y.-Del. and N.J.) $v Remote-sensing images.

651 0 Pennsylvania $v Remote-sensing images.

655 7 Remote-sensing images. $2 lcgft

710 1 United States. $b National Aeronautics and Space Administration.

Record for an Atlas

007   a $b d $d c $e a $f n $g z $h n
010   2013591220
040   DLC $b eng $e rda $c DLC $d OCLCF
020   9789231042270
020   9231042270
034 0   a
050 00   G1046.E15 $b U48 2011
052   3201
049   UPMM
110 2   Unesco.
245 10   From space to place : $b an image atlas of World Heritage sites on the "in danger" list : a collection of satellite images for improved understanding and management of world heritage sites / $c Roger Sayre, U.S. Geological Survey, lead author and manager ; Mario Hernandez, UNESCO, lead advisor and co-author ... [and ten others].
255   Scales differ.
264 1   Paris : $b Published by the United Nations Education, Scientific and Cultural Organization (Unesco) in association with the United States Geological Survey (USGS), $c [2011]
300   1 atlas (82 pages) : $b color illustrations, color maps ; $c 29 x 44 cm
336   cartographic image $2 rdacontent
337   unmediated $2 rdamedia
338   volume $2 rdacarrier
650 0   World Heritage areas $v Maps.
650 0   Endangered ecosystems $v Maps.
650 0   Archaeology $v Maps.
655 7   World atlases. $2 lcgft
655 7   Remote-sensing images. $2 lcgft
700 1   Sayre, Roger, $e author.
710 2   Geological Survey (U.S.)

Record for a Globe

007   d $b c $d c $e a $f n
010   2012587533
040   DLC $b eng $e rda $c DLC $d OCLCQ
034 1   a $b 6700000 $d W1800000 $e E1800000 $f N0900000 $g S0900000
050 00   G3171.C18 1992 $b .R2

052   3171

049   UPMM

110 2   Rand McNally and Company.

245 10 [Seventy-five inch geophysical globe].

255   Scale approximately 1:6,700,000 $c (W 180°--E 180°/N 90°--S 90°).

264 1   [Chicago, Illinois] : $b [Rand McNally and Company], $c [1992]

300   1 globe : $b color, hand-painted, plastic ; $c 190 cm in diameter, mounted on spindle in metal base.

336   cartographic image $b cri $2 rdacontent

337   unmediated $b n $2 rdamedia

338   other $b nz $2 rdacarrier

500   Raised relief globe.

500   Title supplied by cataloger.

500   On permanent display on the second floor mezzanine of the Madison Building of the Library of Congress. $5 DLC

655 7   Globes. $2 lcgft

655 7   Relief models. $2 lcgft

Record for an Online Resource

006   m   o d f

007   a $b r $d c $e z $f n $g z $h n

007   c $b r $d c $e n

040   GPO $b eng $e rda $c GPO $d OCLCO $d GPO $d OCLCQ $d OCLCO $d OCLCA $d GPO $d IUL

034 0   a $d E0673000 $e E0674500 $f N0330000 $g N0324500

043   a-af---

052   7631

052   7633 $b G5 $b Z2

074   0621-K (online)

086 0   I 19.121:709-G

049   UPMM

100 1   Davis, Philip A. $q (Philip Arthur), $d 1950- $e author.

245 10 Local-area-enhanced, 2.5 meter resolution natural-color and color-infrared satellite-image mosaics of the Zarkashan Mineral District in Afghanistan / $c by Philip A. Davis and Laura E. Cagney ; prepared in cooperation with the U.S. Department of Defense Task Force for Business and Stability Operations and the Afghanistan Geological Survey.

255   Scale not given $c (E 67°30'--W 67°45'/N 33°00'--N 32°45').

264 1 [Reston, Va.] : $b U.S. Department of the Interior, U.S. Geological Survey, $c 2012.

300   1 online resource (maps) : $b color.

336   cartographic image $b cri $2 rdacontent

337   computer $b c $2 rdamedia

338   online resource $b cr $2 rdacarrier

490 1 U.S. Geological Survey data series ; $v 709-G

500   Title from title screen (viewed Apr. 1, 2013).

500   Includes index maps and text.

504   Includes bibliographical references.

650 0 Mining districts $z Afghanistan $z Ghaznī $v Remote-sensing images.

650 0 Mining districts $z Afghanistan $z Zābul $v Remote-sensing images.

650 0 Mines and mineral resources $z Afghanistan $z Ghaznī $v Remote-sensing images.

650 0 Mines and mineral resources $z Afghanistan $z Zābul $v Remote-sensing images.

651 0 Zarkashan Mineral District (Afghanistan) $v Remote-sensing images.

655 7 Remote-sensing images. $2 lcgft

700 1 Cagney, Laura E., $e author.

710 2 U.S. Task Force for Business and Stability Operations, $e author.

710 2 Afghan Geological Survey, $e author.

710 2 Geological Survey (U.S.), $e publisher.

830 0 Data series (Geological Survey (U.S.)) ; $v 709-G.

856 40 $u http://pubs.usgs.gov/ds/709/g/

856 40 $u http://purl.fdlp.gov/GPO/gpo35406

Record for a Map on Microfiche

007   h $b e $d b $e m $f u $g z $h u $i u $j u

040   UPM $b eng $e rda $c UPM

034 1 a $b 15840 $d W0811617 $e W0805235 $f N0491910 $g N0485818

050 4 QE191 $b .M36 no.P.774

052   3462 $b C6

052   3461

049   UPMM

110 1 Ontario. $b Division of Mines, $e cartographer.

245 10 Galna Township, District of Cochrane : $b [Ontario] / $c Ontario Division of Mines.

246 1 $i Alternate title in upper left corner: $a Preliminary map P.774 Kirkland Lake Data Series

255   Scale 1:15,840. 1 inch to 1/4 mile $c (W 81°16′17″--W 80°52′35″/N 49°19′10″--N 48°58′18″).

264 1 [Toronto, Ont.] : $b Ministry of Northern Development and Mines, $c [1973]

264 3 [Toronto, Ont.] : $b [Ontario Division of Mines?] $c [198-?]

300   1 microfiche : $b negative ; $c 11 x 15 cm

336   cartographic image $2 rdacontent

337   microform $2 rdamedia

338   microfiche $2 rdacarrier

490 0   Kirkland Lake data series

490 1   Preliminary map ; $v P.774

500   In upper left corner of fiche header: Ontario Ministry of Northern Development and
        Mines.

500   In lower left corner: ODM 4934.

500   "NTS Reference: 42 A/16E."

500   "ODM GSC Aeromagnetic Maps: 2355G."

500   "ODM Geological Compilation Series Map: 2046."

500   "Issued 1972. Corrections and additions (DH) February 1973."

500   Ancillary maps: Data location map -- Provisional geological interpretation -- Surficial
        geology -- Aeromagnetic map.

500   Includes adjoining sheets index map for Kirkland Lake data series sheets, "Metal and
        Mineral Reference List," Sources of Information notes, 4 ancillary maps, data table,
        and descriptive legends.

650 0 Geology $z Ontario $z Cochrane (District) $v Maps.

650 0 Mines and mineral resources $z Ontario $z Cochrane (District) $v Maps.

655 7 Geological maps. $2 lcgft

710 1   Ontario. $b Ministry of Northern Development and Mines.

776 1   ǂc Original. Geological Survey of Canada. $t Galna Township, District of Cochrane. $d
        [Toronto] : Ontario Division of Mines, 1972. $h 1 map ; 59 x 74 cm, folded to 26 x 20
        cm. $w (OCoLC)71504035

830 0   Map (Ontario Geological Survey) ; $v P.774.

Record for a Map Facsimile

007   a $b j $d c $e a $f f $g z $h n

040   UPM $b eng $e rda $c UPM $d UPM

034 0   a $d W1182100 $e W0864200 $f N0324300 $g N0143200

041 0   eng $a spa

042   pcc

043   n-mx---

050 4 G4411.A5 1939 $b .S7 2013

049   UPMM

245 00 Story map of Mexico.

246 1 $i Title below compass rose at lower margin: $a Mejico

255   Scale not given $c (W 118°21'00"--W 86°42'00"/N 32°43'00"--N 14°32'00").

264 3 University Park, Pa. : $b University Libraries, Pennsylvania State University, $c 2013.

300   1 map : $b color ; $c 38 x 51 cm, on sheet 42 x 56 cm

336   cartographic image $2 rdacontent

337   unmediated $2 rdamedia

338   sheet $2 rdacarrier

500   Pictorial map showing peoples, places, ships, vegetation, and so forth surrounded by elaborate border.

500   Relief shown pictorially.

500   Color illustration of "Cathedral Mexico" in upper center border.

500   Also shows the routes of Hernando Cortez, 1519; Don Juan de Grijalva, 1518; Don Hernando de Alarcon, 1540; and 1st Japanese Ambassador to the New World, 1614.

546   In English; some place names in Spanish.

651 0 Mexico $v Maps $v Facsimiles.

655 7 Pictorial maps. $2 lcgft

710 2   Colortext Publications Inc.

775 08 $i Reproduction of (manifestation): $t Story map of Mexico. $d Chicago, Illinois : Colortext Publications, $c 1939. $w (OCoLC)55719057

Record for a Raised Relief Model

007   a $b q $d c $e p $f n $g z $h n

010   2012587567

040   DLC $b eng $e rda $c DLC $d OCLCQ

034 1   a $b 2534400 $c 506880 $d W1250000 $e W0700000 $f N0490000 $g N0250000

043   n-us---

050 00 G3701.C18 1893 $b .H6

052   3701

049   UPMM

100 1   Howell, Edwin E. $q (Edwin Eugene), $d 1845-1911.

245 10 United States and Gulf of Mexico with portions of the Atlantic & Pacific oceans between the 67th and 127th meridians : $b modeled on a section of a globe 16 1/2 ft. in diameter / $c by Edwin E. Howell.

255   Scale 1:2,534,400. Vertical scale 1:506,880. Horizontal scale 1 in. = 40 miles. Vertical scale 1 in. = 8 miles $c (W 125°--W 70°/N 49°--N 25°).

264 3 Washington, D.C. : $b Edwin E. Howell, $c [1893]

300   1 model : $b hand colored, plaster ; $c 123 x 252 x 78 cm, mounted in wooden stand.

336   cartographic image $b cri $2 rdacontent

337   unmediated $b n $2 rdamedia

338   other $b nz $2 rdacarrier

500   Raised relief model.

500   At head of title: United States Geological Survey, J.W. Powell, Director.

651 0 United States $v Maps.

655 7 Relief models. $2 lcgft

655 7 Globes. $2 lcgft

710 2 Geological Survey (U.S.)

Record for Map Series

007   a $b j $d c $e a $f n $g z $h n

040   CGU $b eng $e rda $c CGU $d CGU $d OCLCQ

034 1 a $b 50000 $d E1153000 $e E1184500 $f N0070000 $g N0040000

041 0 may $a eng

043   a-my---

050   4 G8033.S3 s50 $b .G7

052   8033 $b S3

049   UPMM

110 1 Great Britain. $b Directorate of Overseas Surveys.

245 10 Malaysia (Sabah) 1:50,000.

246 1 $i Some sheets have title: $a Malaysia Timor 1:50,000 = $b East Malaysia (Sabah)

246 1 $i Some sheets have title: $a Sabah 1:50,000

246 1 $i Standard map series designation: $a Series T735

255   Scale 1:50,000 ; $b Borneo rectified skew orthomorphic projection $c (E 115°30′--E 118°45′/N 7°00′--N 4°00′).

264 21 [London] : $b Overseas Development Administration (Directorate of Overseas Surveys) for the Director of National Mapping, Malaysia, $c [1965-1974]

264 31 [Kuala Lumpur] : $b Director of National Mapping, $c [1973-1994]

300   maps : $b color ; $c 56 x 56 cm, on sheets 91 x 65 cm

336   cartographic image $b cri $2 rdacontent

337   unmediated $b n $2 rdamedia

338   sheet $b nb $2 rdacarrier

546   Malay and English.

500   Relief shown by contours and spot heights.

500   Older maps are "Published by the Overseas Development Administration (Directorate of Overseas Surveys) for the Director of National Mapping, Malaysia" and "Printed by

the Ordnance Survey." Newer maps are "Published by Director of National Mapping, Malaysia."

500   Each sheet is named and numbered individually, for example: Syit (Sheet) 5/116/1. Kota Kinabalu -- Syit (Sheet) 5/117/4. Gum-Gum.

500   Each sheet includes index to adjoining sheets.

500   "Terhad-Restricted."

651 0 Sabah $v Maps.

655 7 Topographic maps. $2 lcgft

710 1 Malaysia. $b Directorate of National Mapping.

ABOUT THE AUTHORS

PAIGE G. ANDREW is the Maps Cataloging Librarian at the Pennsylvania State University Libraries, holding the rank of Full Librarian. He participates in three of the Library of Congress Program for Cooperative Cataloging (PCC) programs: BIBCO, NACO, and SACO. Mr. Andrew has published articles on the bibliographic control of cartographic materials and related topics in professional journals such as *Cataloging and Classification Quarterly,* and authored *Cataloging Sheet Maps: The Basics* (Haworth Information Press, 2003). He co-edited, with Mary Lynette Larsgaard, *Maps and Related Cartographic Materials: Cataloging, Classification and Bibliographic Control* (Haworth Information Press, 1999), and with Ms. Larsgaard is co-founder of and continues as co-editor of the *Journal of Map and Geography Libraries: Advances in Geospatial Information, Collections and Archives.* Mr. Andrew has served his profession as an officer and as chair of many committees, including those of the Special Libraries Association, the American Library Association, and several others. He continues to share his expertise in map cataloging through workshops given at conferences and individual institutions as well as through formal presentations. He was the recipient of the 2009 Nancy B. Olson Award for significant contributions to audiovisual cataloging by OLAC (Online Audiovisual Catalogers, Inc.). His MLS is from the University of Washington and BA from Western Washington University (Geography).

SUSAN M. MOORE is a Catalog Librarian and Bibliographer at the Rod Library at the University of Northern Iowa in Cedar Falls, Iowa. She has been teaching map cataloging workshops since 1999. She is a member of the Map and Geospatial Information Round Table (MAGIRT) of the American Library Association. She currently chairs the MAGIRT Committee on Cataloging and Classification and is the MAGIRT liaison to the Library of Congress' MARC Advisory Committee. Ms. Moore received the MAGIRT Honors Award in 2009. Her MLS is from the University of Iowa and she earned an MA in Geography from the University of Arizona.

MARY LYNETTE LARSGAARD is Librarian Emeritus of the UCSB Libraries. She was formerly Assistant Head and then Head of the Map and Imagery Laboratory, Davidson Library, University of California at Santa Barbara. She holds a BA in Geology from Macalester College, an MA in Library Science from the University of Minnesota, and an MA in Geography from the University of Oregon. Ms. Larsgaard has published extensively in the field of cartographic resources in libraries, most notably *Map Librarianship: An Introduction* (third edition, Libraries Unlimited, 1998). Her specialties are cataloging/metadata creation, and collection development and other aspects of twentieth-century and more recent topographic and geologic maps.

INDEX